shine

shine

screenplay by jan sardi
story by scott hicks

BLOOMSBURY

David and Gillian
for sharing your lives with us.

First published in Great Britain 1997

Copyright © 1997 Momentum Films Pty Ltd

The moral right of the author has been asserted

Bloomsbury Publishing Plc, 38 Soho Square, London W1V 5DF

A CIP catalogue record for this book
is available from the British Library

10   9   8   7   6   5   4   3   2

ISBN 0 7475 3173 0

Typeset by Hewer Text Composition Services, Edinburgh
Printed in Great Britain by St Edmundsbury Press, Suffolk

Preface

When I first saw David Helfgott perform I had no idea
that I was about to embark on a ten year odyssey. But
through the decade of developing the screenplay and
making the film, David's story remained inspirational –
the triumph of light at the end of the tunnel. This was the
feeling that had struck me so forcefully that night in 1986.

And through this most particular of lives ran
powerful and universal themes: the story of a boy who
is never allowed to grow up, and who becomes a 40
year-old child prodigy; and of a father; driven by
overpowering love and a history that compels him to
hold his family together at all costs, who simply cannot
part with the little genius he has created.

Shine is David's journey to define his individuality. His
character finds it hard to discern where he 'ends' and other
people 'begin'. So he 'flows' around others, a babbling river
of words who only seems defined through his virtuosity.
Perhaps the gift of prodigy comes with this inherent risk
that one small sliver of personality can be developed to the
exclusion of other elements that create a complete person.

For me these ideas lay outside the structures of
diagnosis, therapy, and the clinical – the TV 'movie of the
week' fare. Rather the power and the poetry of the story
lay in the emotional journey of an artist who finds himself
consumed by the very medium he is struggling to conquer.

At the same time, everything in the story has its touch-
stone in reality. Despite the usual condensations, compressed
chronology and elements of invention *Shine* remains true to
the emotional journey of David Helfgott's life.

Scott Hicks – Director

INTRODUCTION

Parkes
Your hands must form the unbreakable habit of
playing the notes so you can forget them and let
this take over.

(the heart . . .)

That's where it comes from.

It was in 1990 that Scott Hicks first approached me to
write the screenplay for a film on the life of pianist
David Helfgott which he had been developing for
several years. I was immediately taken by Scott's
passion. Looking back now, I am grateful to have had
the opportunity to share in it and be inspired by it over
the many years it took to bring *Shine* to the screen.

The challenge *Shine* presented was to find a way to
tell this remarkable story – it spans three decades – in
the space of a hundred minutes while remaining faithful
to the essence of the biographical facts. I had to learn
the 'notes' (so to speak) and then forget them and let
the story-teller in me take over.

A strong emotional line is what drives a film or play
and engages an audience in a way that was essential for
Shine to work. Screenwriting manuals will tell you the
shorter the time frame in which a story takes place the
better. David's real-life story covers three decades and
an enormous range of characters, relationships and

incidents, all of which threw up the usual problems and pitfalls of the 'bio-pic' genre which we assiduously wanted to avoid. The key, we both agreed, was to create a strong emotional line.

It was also important for the story to move rapidly, for developments to take place 'in between' scenes, allowing the audience to participate by having to fill it in for themselves. It's a way of letting the audience step into the world of the film. Another way is to rely more on visuals to tell the story as opposed to dialogue. It means at times the script can look spare on the page but it is just the 'blueprint', not the building.

Over the five years and numerous drafts that Scott and I collaborated as writer and director, the process of refinement was constant and continued not only into production but also into post-production. The draft of the script that follows is the 'shooting script'. It contains everything that was shot in the course of production. It is not the post-production script.

Jan Sardi – Screenwriter

CAST

PETER	ARMIN MUELLER-STAHL
DAVID AS A YOUNG MAN	NOAH TAYLOR
DAVID AS AN ADULT	GEOFFREY RUSH
GILLIAN	LYNN REDGRAVE
SYLVIA	SONIA TODD
KATHERINE SUSANNAH PRICHARD	GOOGIE WITHERS
CECIL PARKES	JOHN GIELGUD
BEN ROSEN	NICHOLAS BELL
SAM	CHRIS HAYWOOD
RACHEL	MARTA KACZMAREK
DAVID AS A CHILD	ALEX RAFALOWICZ

and in order of appearance

TONY	JUSTIN BRAINE
EISTEDDFOD PRESENTER	GORDON POOLE
SUZIE AS A CHILD	DANIELLE COX
MARGARET	REBECCA GOODEN
JIM MINOGUE	JOHN COUSINS
STATE CHAMPION ANNOUNCER	PAUL LINKSON
ISAAC STERN	RANDALL BERGER
BOY NEXT DOOR	IAN WELBOURN
LOUISE AS A BABY	KELLY BOTTRILL
RABBI	BEVERLEY VAUGHAN
SYNAGOGUE SECRETARY	PHYLLIS BURFORD
SOCIETY HOSTESS	DAPHNE GREY
SOVIET SOCIETY SECRETARY	EDWIN HODGEMAN
SONIA	MARIA DAFNERO
POSTMAN	REIS PORTER
ROGER WOODWARD (YOUNGER)	STEPHEN SHEEHAN

ANNOUNCER	BRENTON WHITTLE
SUZIE AS A TEENAGER	MARIANNA DOHERTY
LOUISE AS A CHILD	CAMILLA JAMES
VINEY	DAVID KING
REGISTRAR	DANNY DAVIES
SARAH	HELEN DOWELL
MURIEL	LOUISE DORLING
STUDENT	SEAN CARLSEN
ASHLEY	RICHARD HANSELL
ROBERT	ROBERT HANDS
RAY	MARC WARREN
RCOM CONDUCTOR	NEIL THOMSON
SUZIE AS AN ADULT	JOEY KENNEDY
NURSE	ELLEN CRESSEY
BERYL ALCOTT	BEVERLEY DUNN
BAR CUSTOMER	ANDY SEYMOUR
JESSICA	ELLA SCOTT LYNCH
ROWAN	JETHRO HEYSEN-HICKS
ROGER WOODWARD (OLDER)	JOHN MARTIN
CELEBRANT	BILL BOYLEY
OPERA SINGERS	TERESA LA ROCCA
	LINDSEY DAY
	GRANT DOYLE
MUSICIANS	LEAH JENNINGS
	KATHY MONAGHAN
	MARK LAWRENCE
	GORDON COOMBES
	LUKE DOLLMAN
	MARGARET STONE
	TOM CARRIG
	HELEN AYRES
VOCALISTS	SUZI JARRATT
	SAMANTHA MCDONALD

HAND DOUBLE FOR NOAH TAYLOR	MARTIN COUSIN
HAND DOUBLE FOR ALEX RAFALOWICZ	SIMON TEDESCHI
HAND DOUBLE FOR GEOFFREY RUSH	HIMSELF

Overleaf: SCOTT HICKS, DIRECTOR

SHINE

1 INT. TRANSIT LOUNGE. AIRPORT. NIGHT.

DAVID HELFGOTT *wakes with a start in an indistinct place somewhere in the world. Late thirties, eyelids at half-mast, he stares into the wet night, mesmerised by a flashing red light.*

DAVID (*mumbling*): Kissed them all, I kissed them all, always kissed cats, puss-cats, kissed them, always did; if a cat'd let me kiss it, I'd kiss it – Cat on a fence I'll kiss it – always, always, I will didn't I? I did because I was different wasn't I, I was – gotta be different again, haven't I darl –

He realises the seat beside him is empty and panics.

DAVID: Where-oh-where, Gillian? Where did she go, where-oh –

His weird behaviour draws attention.

GILLIAN (*returning*): It's alright David, I'm right here.

DAVID: Here – here Gillian, right here. The thing is I thought you were gone.

She emanates calmness, warmth and is an endless source of energy. The effect is instantaneous. DAVID *settles . . .*

GILLIAN: Where is there to go?

DAVID: I don't know darling, I don't know, I'm hopeless without my glasses.

GILLIAN: You've got your contacts in, silly.

DAVID: I'm a silly, it's true, it's true.

A braying laugh.

Whooahh!

GILLIAN: Shhhh.

DAVID: Oooh, shhh – shhh, sorry darling, sorry –

GILLIAN: It's alright. Stretch your legs.

DAVID: Do you think so? Perhaps I should, perhaps I should stretch my legs, should I stretch my legs?

He stands.

GILLIAN: Good idea.

DAVID: Good idea, that's right –

AIRPORT ANNOUNCEMENT: Flight 313 to London via Frankfurt will be re-boarding in 15 minutes –

DAVID: Whooahhh, London, Gillian, London!

GILLIAN: Yes . . . Shhh.

DAVID: Shhh . . .

He looks out the rain-spattered window at the flashing red light from an aircraft being fuelled immediately outside the window.

DAVID: Shhh, softly, softly, new story . . .

Dissolve to iridescent neon raindrops coursing down a window in the night somewhere. Suddenly a desperate face fills the frame. It's DAVID *in his late twenties. The full head of hair, falling around his soaking wet face, tells us this is years earlier; a sodden cigarette hangs from his lips, spectacles dangle off the end of his nose. He's looking into . . .*

2 INT/EXT. MOBY'S WINEBAR. NIGHT.

A pianist croons the last few bars of 'Only the Lonely'. A waiter, TONY, *shows the last two patrons to the door.* TONY *and a woman in her mid-forties,* SYLVIA, *put up chairs; the* PIANIST, SAM, *slips into a stool at the bar. They chat but all we hear is* DAVID'S *anxious breathing as we are seeing it all from his POV. He raps on the window.*

SYLVIA: What does he want?

SAM: A drink probably. Get lost!

DAVID *disappears from the window and appears at the door.*

SYLVIA: Poor thing. Let him in.

TONY: He's a derro'!

SYLVIA: He's saturated.

Resume DAVID'S *POV as more words are exchanged then* TONY *comes over and opens the door to him.*

TONY: What's the problem, mate?

3

DAVID (*a hundred miles an hour*): Sorry, sorry, sorry, mate, I'm the problem, I think I'm the problem, such a problem. And wet! But it's not an ideal world. Is it an ideal world? We just have to make the most of it, I mean, this is the way we find it isn't it, yeah-yeah-yeah! But it's more ideal than it was, I mean, you know, we're privileged, we're privileged, we're privileged, aren't we, because not long ago, people would be burned to a steak wouldn't they, er . . .

He sees 'MOBY'S' embroidered on TONY's *tunic.*

DAVID: Moby, yay Moby, pleased to meet you –

TONY: Tony. Who are you?

DAVID (*hugs Tony*): Tony, Tony not Moby Tony. Who am I Tony? Who knows Tony? I don't know myself. Whooahh! David, I'm David, I'm David Tony . . . How does that sound?

SYLVIA: Hello David. How can Sylvia help?

DAVID: Sylvia? Is it Sylvia? How are you Sylvia? Good to see you, Sylvia.

He throws an arm around her neck as though greeting a long-lost friend.

DAVID: Sylvia Tony, Tony Sylvia.

SYLVIA: What can we do for you, David?

DAVID: Do for me, Sylvia, what, yes, got to stop talking, got to stop, got to stop, it's a problem isn't it? Is it a problem?

SYLVIA: It's alright David; just tell Sylvia why you're here.

DAVID: Ahhhh! Well it's a mystery, a mystery, a mystery –

SYLVIA: Are you lost?

DAVID: Am I lost? Perhaps that's it. I'm lost, I'm lost, I'm lost. How does that sound?

He sees the piano.

Ooh you have a piano. Is that your piano, Sylvia? Beautiful Sylvia. Isn't Sylvia beautiful Tony? You too Tony. Perhaps I could play it. Could I play it? You say, you say.

SAM: Like hell baby.

SYLVIA: Shut up, Sam.

DAVID (*lurches towards* SAM): Hell baby, the Devil, Diablerie Sam baby!

SAM: Get outta here.

TONY *is in fits of laughter . . .*

SYLVIA: David –

DAVID: Sylvia, such a beautiful piano exquisite Sylvia, Sylvia-Tony –

He moves towards it.

Could I play, you say, you say?

SYLVIA: Why don't you tell Sylvia where you live?

DAVID: Live, Sylvia, live – live and let live – that's very important isn't it? Molto, molto. But then again it's a lifelong struggle, isn't it Sylvia-Tony, to live, to survive, to survive undamaged and not destroy any

5

living breathing creature. The point is, if you do something wrong you can be punished for the rest of your life so I think it's a lifelong struggle; is it a lifelong struggle? Whatever you do it's a struggle, a struggle to keep your head above water and not get it chopped off. I'm not disappointing you am I Sylvia-Tony-Moby-Sam, yay Sam!

3 EXT. STREETS. NIGHT.

SYLVIA's *old Humber belts past in the heavy rain.*

4 INT. SYLVIA'S CAR. NIGHT.

TONY *is driving.* SYLVIA *is in front, both laughing along with* DAVID *in the back.*

DAVID (*a braying laugh*): 'Helfgott' – 'with the help of God' – that's what it means Sylvia. How's that? You see, Daddy's daddy was religious, vee-eery religious, very strict; and a bit of a meanie. But he got exterminated, didn't he, so God didn't help him. Whooahhh. Not very funny is it, Sylvia? Very sad, really sad – I'm callous aren't I, such a meanie because I haven't got a soul, is that right – that's right isn't it?

SYLVIA (O/S): What do you mean?

DAVID: Daddy, daddy said so. No such thing as a soul.

A train whistle sounds in the distance.

SYLVIA: That's ridiculous.

DAVID: Ridiculous; you're right. I'm ridiculous Sylvia-

Tony, and callous Daddy said because it was a tragedy, a tragedy . . .

The car drives into a tunnel. Blackness in the tunnel.

DAVID (V/O): . . . a ridiculous tragedy.

The sound of the train wheels rattling, blasting a signal sweeps us into bright light.

7 INT. OLD HALL. DAY.

As if in a dream, children's faces turn to look at camera in soundless slow-motion. Some are made up, prissy, perfectly dressed for a performance, accompanied by 'stage mothers', fanning themselves in the stifling heat, all eyes focused on the next contestant as he makes his way up the centre aisle. His POV. Over this we fade up.

ANNOUNCER: Let's hear it for our next young contestant, David Helfgott.

DAVID, *nine, makes his way down the aisle clutching a score. His hair is meticulously parted and he wears spectacles. A little uncertain, he stops and looks back to his father.* PETER HELFGOTT *is a thickset Polish man in his fifties. He motions for* DAVID *to keep going, then sits, anxious and excited.* DAVID *walks up some steps onto the stage.*

ANNOUNCER: David's going to play the piano for us, aren't you David?

DAVID: Yes.

He's stage-struck by all those faces looking at him, including three judges – two elderly females and a man in his thirties. His name is BEN ROSEN.

7

ANNOUNCER: What are you going to play?

DAVID's *attention is taken by a fan nearby, blades whirring.*

ANNOUNCER: David, what are you going to play?

DAVID *snaps out of it, when from the audience . . .*

PETER (*stands*): Chopin! The Polonaise!

PETER *smiles full of charm, and a little embarrassed at all eyes on him; he applauds encouragingly then sits.*

DAVID's *heels click on the bare boards as he crosses to the old upright piano centre-stage. He adjusts his music. His bony legs barely reach the pedals. He fidgets, looks into the spotlight. He takes a deep breath, then launches into Chopin's Polonaise in A Flat, the first few bars ring out with unusual power, surprising everyone –* BEN ROSEN *in particular.*

DAVID *attacks the keys with such gusto that the piano inches forward. He hooks his foot around the leg of the stool and drags it in. He plays on. The piano moves again. He blurs some notes. Again he readjusts the stool without missing a beat; pages of his score flutter to the ground but* DAVID *plays on, undaunted, to the end.* ROSEN *watches the courageous performance with wry amazement.* PETER *arrives backstage flustered. To the* ANNOUNCER:

PETER: The piano, it is disgraceful.

The piano slews forward. DAVID *stands and plays the final few bars with awesome intensity.*

ANNOUNCER: This kid's good; he's great.

A moment.

PETER: He's my son!

8 EXT. HELFGOTT HOUSE. DAY.

The expectant faces of two young girls loom large as they look down the street from their perch in a tree – MARGARET, *12, and* SUZIE, *5.*

SUZIE: Did he win or lose?

Along the street, DAVID *walks a few paces behind* PETER.

MARGARET: He lost.

DAVID *jumps over the cracks in the pavement.*

MARGARET: Now we'll all cop it. Damn you David Helfgott.

9 INT. HELFGOTT HOUSE. DAY.

PETER *broods, his mind turning over. A scratchy recording of Rachmaninov's Third Piano Concerto plays on the gramophone.* DAVID *moves a chess piece and waits for* PETER.

RACHEL HELFGOTT, PETER's *wife, lights the woodstove. Her face, once beautiful, is now blanketed by the hollow look of years of submission.* MARGARET *is doing homework on the kitchen table.*

DAVID: It's your turn, Daddy.

PETER *flicks a look at the board and moves a piece.*

PETER: You know, David, when I was your age, I bought a violin, I saved for that violin, it was a beautiful violin. *All listen to the story they've heard before.* Do you know what happened to it?

DAVID *glances at a photo of a stern rabbi high up on the wall.*

9

DAVID: He smashed it.

A moment, then PETER *slams his fist on the small table, knocking some chess pieces off.*

PETER: You are a lucky boy. My father never let me have music.

DAVID: I know, Daddy.

PETER: You are very lucky.

DAVID: Yes Daddy. (*Lights up.*) Will I play for you?

PETER: No. You pick up these pieces.

DAVID *proceeds to on hands and knees while* PETER *goes to switch the gramophone off.*

MARGARET (*to* DAVID): I bet I could've won.

PETER (*in Yiddish*): Quiet.

DAVID *pokes a face at* MARGARET. *She does the same to him, careful for* PETER *not to see.* DAVID *gallops the knight across the board. There's a knock at the front door.* MARGARET *makes to go.*

PETER: Margaret!

She stops.

I told you, tell your friends not to come.

She sits. There's another knock which PETER *ignores.*

10 EXT. HELFGOTT HOUSE. SIDEWAY. DAY.

BEN ROSEN *walks around the sideway of the dilapidated*

old house, uncertain if there's anyone home. He spots someone in the backyard.

ROSEN: Hello.

It's SUZIE.

SUZIE: Hello.

ROSEN: Who are you?

11 INT/EXT. HELFGOTT HOUSE. BACKYARD. DAY.

PETER *looks across.*

SUZIE (*O/S*): Daddy, there's someone here.

ROSEN *appears at the back door.*

ROSEN: I hope I'm not interupting . . .

PETER *stands in the doorway looking down at him, resenting the intrusion.*

ROSEN: Ben Rosen. I was one of the judges.

PETER *doesn't accept the proffered handshake. He motions* SUZIE *in.*

PETER (*to* ROSEN): Yes?

ROSEN: You left before all the prizes were announced.

DAVID *appears behind* PETER.

ROSEN: You were very good this afternoon, David.

DAVID: Thank you.

PETER: He can play better.

ROSEN: Maybe he was a little too good. Some people don't like that. We gave him a special prize for his courage.

PETER *takes the envelope from* ROSEN *and peels it open.* MARGARET *starts playing the piano in the background.*

ROSEN: It was a very difficult piece you chose, David.

DAVID: Daddy chose it.

ROSEN *notices* RACHEL *sneak a look out the window at him.*

ROSEN: Even great pianists think twice before tackling the Polonaise

DAVID's *eyes light up as* PETER *takes a pound note from the envelope.*

PETER: A prize for losing!

He pockets the money.

ROSEN: I wouldn't call him a loser.

PETER (*in Yiddish, to* MARGARET): Stop, that is enough!

She stops playing.

ROSEN (*in Yiddish*): She plays well too.

The Yiddish catches PETER *out.*

PETER (*disdainful*): They all play.

ROSEN: I'm quite sure David could win lots of competitions with the right tuition.

He offers a business card showing his qualifications.

PETER: I teach him.

ROSEN: You've obviously done well.

PETER: Yes – and no on taught me; no music teachers Mr Rosen.

ROSEN: Of course, it's just that a few bad habits can sometimes mean the difference between winning or losing.

He knows which strings to pull.

If you'd like to think about it.

He hands PETER *the card.* PETER *holds his look and closes the door on him.*

12 EXT. STREET OUTSIDE HELFGOTT HOUSE. NIGHT.

The house is in darkness.

13 INT. HELFGOTT HOUSE. NIGHT.

In the bedroom PETER *wakes to the sound of the piano filtering through from the living area.*

He walks down the hallway, drawn by the sparse, haunting music which is familiar: Rachmaninov's Third Piano Concerto. Entering the living area he sees DAVID *playing the piano in near darkness.* DAVID *struggles to get his small fingers across the keys, faltering to a stop . . .*

PETER: Rachmaninov?

DAVID: It's beautiful.

PETER *sits beside his son.*

PETER: You taught yourself?

DAVID: From the record.

PETER: The record?

DAVID: You always play it.

PETER *smiles.*

PETER: It is very difficult, the hardest piece in the world, David.

DAVID: Will you teach me?

Pause. PETER *deflects.*

PETER: One day you will play it, you will make me very proud.

PETER *hugs his small son.*

PETER: Next time, what are we going to do?

DAVID: We're going to win.

PETER: We're going to win! (*Kisses him.*) Now go to bed.

DAVID: Goodnight, Daddy.

Moments later PETER *takes a score from a battered suitcase full of music: Rachmaninov's Third Piano Concerto. It's awesome in its complexity, page after page.* PETER *positions it on the piano, then contemplates the keys with his own thickset, clumsy hands. The framed photo of the rabbi looks down at him.* PETER *clenches his fists in frustration.*

14 EXT. BEN ROSEN'S HOUSE. DAY.

DAVID *and* PETER *walk along a cobbled path.* DAVID *stops to look at some goldfish in a large pond.* PETER *bustles him along to the front door of the house. Rain threatens.* PETER *rings the bell.* DAVID *smiles and goes to do the same but* PETER *stops him with a look.*

The door is opened by ROSEN.

PETER: I have decided I would like you to teach David. (*Hands him some music.*) This!

ROSEN: Rachmaninov? Don't be ridiculous.

PETER: He can play it already.

ROSEN: He's just a boy. How can he express that sort of passion?

PETER: You are a passionate man, Mr Rosen. You will teach him, no?

ROSEN: No. I'll teach him what I think is best.

DAVID *is entranced by some chimes hanging over his head.*

PETER: Rachmaninov is best. (*No response.*) But you are his teacher; I let you decide.

ROSEN (*dry*): Thank you. We'll start with Mozart.

He lets DAVID *in and* PETER *goes to follow but the door is already closing on him.*

PETER: I can't afford to pay.

The door shuts, leaving PETER *stranded. It starts to rain. The sound of scales issues from inside.*

15 INT. ROSEN'S HOUSE. DAY.

DAVID *plays the scales.* ROSEN *spots* PETER *at the side window, peering in.* ROSEN *shuts the blind on him.*

16 EXT. ROSEN'S SIDEWAY.

PETER, *in the rain, presses his ear to the window. The sound of thunder advanced from*:

17 EXT. LODGE. NIGHT. THE PRESENT.

Heavy rain. Sylvia's car pulls up. She jumps out and opens the back door.

SYLVIA: Come on David, Sylvia's getting wet.

She drags him out.

DAVID: Wet Sylvia, sorry Sylvia, such a wet.

They run past a sign clanging on a chain: 'Eden Lodge'.

18 INT. DAVID'S ROOM AT EDEN LODGE. NIGHT.

SYLVIA *is appalled by what she sees. The room is littered with sheet music, rubbish, cigarette butts.*

SYLVIA: Is this your room, David?

DAVID: It's a room, it's a room, home sweet home.

She looks at the piano – a battered honky-tonk, chipped keys all burnt by cigarettes.

SYLVIA: You can play?

DAVID: Kind of, kind of play kind of sweet kind Sylvia.
(*Picks up sheet music.*) Chopin, Sylvia, Chopinzee!
The Pole-popolski. Like Daddy and his family before
they were concentrated.

He brushes a Rachmaninov score aside.

SYLVIA: How long have you been here?

DAVID: Golly, I don't know. Aeons I think, a few years, a
few. And Schubert, nothing wrong with Schubert
except syphilis, was it syphilis? I think it was. Then
he got typhoid on top of it and that was the end of
him wasn't it? We lost him –

She notices a row of tablet bottles by the bed.

DAVID: That was a bit careless wasn't it Sylvia – Whooah
we lost him, we lost him, didn't live to swim another
day.

MINOGUE *enters; late fifties, he has a thick Scottish
accent and a suspicious look in his eye.*

DAVID: Jim. I was a naughty boy wasn't I? Was I a
naughty boy? Chop chop, off with the head.

MINOGUE: I was about to send out a search party.

He shuts the window.

DAVID: Whooahhh, a search party Jim, a party! I won't
be invited again, will I Sylvia?

SYLVIA: He showed up at my restaurant, seemed a bit
lost.

DAVID: How's that Sylvia, how's that? A party! A
    celebration. A fiesta – !

MINOGUE: He's good at that. Thank you for bringing him
    back.

He ushers her out.

DAVID: Time for a wine and a very fine time. A mardi
    gras and a nice long cigar – Whoooah Jim Jim Jim, a
    party.

*He realises he's on his own. He stares blankly at the
rain hitting the window, getting louder until it becomes
the sound of applause, from:*

19 INT. CONCERT HALL. DAY. THE PAST.

Rows of enthusiastic clapping hands.

PRESENTER (V/O): The winner and State champion,
    David Helfgott.

*As the wild applause continues, we end on a big close-
up of DAVID as he comes up from a bow, now a young
adolescent. Several years have passed.*

20 INT. HELFGOTT HOUSE. DAY.

SUZIE: He won! David won!

MARGARET: I can hear that. I'm not deaf.

RACHEL *nurses baby* LOUISE.

RACHEL: That's your clever brother.

20

21 INT. BACKSTAGE OF HALL.

PETER *bursts through the door, rushes up to* ROSEN *and kisses him on both cheeks.*

PETER: We won. We won.

ROSEN: Thanks to Mozart.

PETER: Now he can play Rachmaninov.

ROSEN *sighs.* DAVID *takes centre stage.* PETER *watches from the wings with* ROSEN *and the other contestants.*

PRESENTER: And now to present David with the prize money, our very special guest from America, ladies and gentlemen, currently on tour in Australia – Isaac Stern.

STERN *shakes hands with* DAVID. PETER *applauds vigorously, overwhelmed with excitement.*

PETER: He's my son!

STERN (*to* DAVID): You have a very special talent, David.

DAVID: Thank you, thank you Mr Stern. So do you.

Laughter.

STERN: How much are you prepared to give to your music, David?

DAVID: How much?

PETER (*from the wings*): Everything.

ROSEN *settles* PETER.

21

DAVID: Everything. But I do like tennis – and chemistry too.

Laughter. PETER *laughs too.*

STERN: Do you play tennis as well as you play Mozart?

DAVID: Only against the wall at home, I bounce the ball against the wall mainly.

STERN: How would you like to come to a special school in the States where music bounces off the walls?

DAVID*'s imagination is captured.*

DAVID: America?

STERN: Land of the Free. Home of the Brave! You know?

PETER*'s expression falters.*

PRESENTER: Ladies and gentlemen, what an honour for our young state champion to be invited to study in America.

The audience applauds. People congratulate PETER.

ROSEN: That's fantastic, Peter.

PETER *applauds enthusiastically despite the uncomfortable feeling inside he is yet to fully understand.* DAVID *beams into the audience, soaking up that winning feeling. Fade to white:*

SUZIE'S VOICE*: 'And now, all the way from America, David Helfgott.'*

23 EXT. HELFGOTT HOUSE. BACKYARD. DAY.

DAVID *steps out from behind bright white sheets hanging on the line and bows repeatedly to an imaginary audience.*

MARGARET: He's not *from* America.

She takes the washing off the line. The yard is crammed with empty bottles and scrap metal.

SUZIE: He's going *to* America and when he comes *back* he'll be coming *from* there, won't you David?

DAVID *bows still, until* MARGARET *unpegs the sheet.*

SUZIE: Aren't you going to miss him?

MARGARET: Yes.

DAVID *smiles as he realises she means it.*

DAVID: Me too.

YOUTH'S VOICE: Margaret.

MARGARET *puts the washing down and exits the back gate.*

24 INT. HELFGOTT HOUSE. KITCHEN. DAY.

PETER: I have no money to send David to America.

ROSEN: We'll raise it.

PETER *scoffs.* RACHEL *looks over from the sink where she's scraping marrow from bones into a pot.*

23

ROSEN: Bar mitzvah.

PETER: What?

ROSEN: David hasn't had his bar mitzvah.

PETER *looks out the window.*

PETER: Religion is nonsense.

ROSEN: It's also a goldmine if you know where to dig.

25 EXT. HELFGOTT HOUSE. BACKYARD. DAY.

DAVID: One day I'll play with an orchestra.

SUZIE: Can I come when you do?

DAVID: You can ride with me in my cadillac.

SUZIE: Where are you going to live in America?

Behind them, PETER *steps out of the kitchen.*

DAVID: With a nice Jewish family they said.

PETER: And this is not a nice family?

DAVID: Oh yes, very nice, very –

PETER: You are very lucky to have a family!

He stabs a look at the abandoned laundry basket – no sign of MARGARET.

26 EXT. HELFGOTT HOUSE. REAR LANEWAY. DAY.

PETER's *face appears over the rear corrugated iron fence*

which has a strand of barbed wire running across the top. In the laneway MARGARET *is talking to a* GANGLY YOUTH. *Seeing* PETER *she pales.*

MARGARET: I have to go.

She hurries to the gate. When she opens it, PETER *is there. She squashes past him, his eyes burning through her.*

27 INT. HELFGOTT KITCHEN. DAY.

ROSEN: It's one of the finest music schools in the world.

RACHEL: It is for his father to decide.

ROSEN: David will be well looked after, I assure you.

RACHEL *nods politely, unconvinced.*

Pause.

ROSEN *(perplexed, steps closer)*: Rachel, David could well be one of the truly great pianists.

RACHEL: He is just a boy, Mr Rosen. He still wets the bed.

ROSEN *absorbs this.* MARGARET *fumes past.*

28 EXT. STREET. DAY.

A rickety pram wheel wobbles along. Widen to reveal PETER *pushing the dilapidated old pram down the ordinary suburban street, flanked by* DAVID *and* SUZIE *wearing grubby school uniforms.*

Several kids playing hopscotch stop as they see them approaching, then clear a path for the odd trio to pass. SUZIE *looks down her nose at them.* DAVID *performs the hopscotch without missing a beat as the trio continues on its way. The kids watch after them, like they were from another planet.*

Wide shot. DAVID *and* SUZIE *collect several bottles which have been left on the sidewalk, put them in the pram and walk on with* PETER.

30 EXT. HELFGOTT HOUSE. BACKYARD. DAY.

PETER *straddles a large piece of scrap metal – the head of a truck engine – and heaves it off the pram with a great sense of satisfaction. It joins a pile of metal and a stack of empty bottles in the corner of the yard.*

PETER: You see how fit I am, you see how strong?

SUZIE: Show me Daddy, show me where the lion scratched you when you worked at the circus.

PETER *extends his hand with a sense of theatricality to reveal a long, jagged scar.*

PETER: That's what happens when you get too close to the bars.

He stands in a body-builder pose, barrel-chested.

PETER: Come on David, hit me.

SUZIE: Me!

PETER: David, as hard as you can.

27

DAVID: Okay. Here comes. Ready.

DAVID's *punch bounces off* PETER's *stomach.*

SUZIE: My turn Daddy.

PETER: Harder. Come on! (DAVID *punches again.*) You
see. A man of steel.

DAVID: Steel alright. (*Rubbing his fist.*)

PETER: No one can hurt me! Because in this world only
the fit survive.

RACHEL *watches from the laundry, sweating over the
hot copper; she sees another side to the fun and games.*

PETER: The weak get crushed like insects. Believe me, if
you want to survive in America you have to be fit and
strong, like me.

31 INT. SYNAGOGUE. OFFICE CORRIDOR. DAY.

*An elderly receptionist types with one finger on an
antiquated typewriter.* PETER *sits in the narrow corridor,
arms folded tightly. He would rather be somewhere else.
On the wall opposite him a long line of faces – the
portraits of past rabbis of the synagogue stare down.*

PETER *glances at the folded newspaper on the seat next
to him:* The Maccabean. *On the front page – a photo of*
DAVID *seated at the piano with a smiling* PETER,
pointing at a score as if taking DAVID *through a lesson.*

*The elderly typist removes the sheet from the typewriter
and smiles at* PETER. *He nods politely, then resumes his*

steely composure. The door to the RABBI'*s office opens.*
PETER *stands.*

RABBI (*exits the office with David*): See you next week
    David, and don't forget to study. (He hands him the
    'soncino chumash'.) We'll see you in Schul, Elias.

PETER *feigns a polite smile.*

DAVID: Thank you Rabbi.

They walk off. DAVID *takes* The Maccabean *from him,
noting the stand displaying more copies of this latest
issue.* PETER *puts his arm on* DAVID'*s shoulder, draws
him in, as if protecting him from an invisible foe. The*
RABBI *considers it, then goes back into his office.*

34 EXT. HELFGOTT HOUSE. DAY.

The POSTMAN *rides along the street, past* DAVID *waiting
expectantly at his front gate. No mail today.*

DAVID *watches after him, sighs.*

35 INT. BOKSER MANSION. NIGHT.

A chandelier glistens above the entry. DAVID *and* PETER
*enter tentatively. The foyer is dripping with dignity and
provincial social elite.* DAVID *and* PETER *are immediately
set on by the hostess,* MRS BOKSER, *a busy socialite.*

MRS BOKSER: Mr Helfgott, it's exciting isn't it? David, the
    Lord Mayor's dying to meet you.

29

She takes DAVID *by the hand, dragging him away. A* WAITER *offers* PETER *a drink from a tray but* PETER'*s attention is on* DAVID *being whisked away.*

Cut to a short while later. Faces glowing with appreciation and sparkling jewellery surround DAVID.

MRS BOKSER: And I would like to thank our wonderful Lord Mayor for establishing this fund for David to go to America.

(*Applause.*)

And now to play for us, our very own David Helfgott.

ROSEN *notes* PETER'*s embittered look around the room as the gathering smothers* DAVID *with affection on his way to the piano – a shake of the hand, a kiss, etc.*

36 EXT. HELFGOTT HOUSE. NIGHT.

PETER'*s voice can be heard raging inside.*

PETER (V/O): These people are a disgrace!

37 INT. HELFGOTT HOUSE. GIRLS' BEDROOM. NIGHT.

SUZIE *nestles up to* MARGARET *and baby* LOUISE, *frightened by the yelling.*

PETER (V/O): A disgrace. (*A loud thump.*) They think they are so important. (*Curses in Yiddish.*)

38 INT. HELFGOTT HOUSE. LOUNGE. NIGHT.

PETER *paces, like a caged lion, bursting with anger.*

PETER: What do they know with their furs and their diamonds? It makes me sick to the stomach.

RACHEL *is on the receiving end.*

PETER: And Rosen. Pah!

39 INT. DAVID'S ROOM. NIGHT.

DAVID *lies in bed listening.*

PETER (V/O): What kind of man is he? He has no children. He's not married, I know! Don't talk to me about Rosen.

40 INT. HELFGOTT HOUSE. LOUNGE. NIGHT.

PETER *curses again in Yiddish.*

RACHEL: He only wants for David the same as you have always wanted.

PETER: Don't ever compare me to him. What has he suffered? Not a day in his life! What does he know about families? Do you forget how your sisters died?

He thumps the wall by the photograph of RACHEL *and her sisters.*

PETER: And my mother and father. (*Yiddish.*) Stupid woman. Stupid!

Cut to later. PETER *sits in near darkness, just staring it seems. We realise he is looking at a scrapbook, articles and photos of* DAVID *throughout his brief but stunning career, including a photo with Isaac Stern.*

PETER *stares, his mind turning the same thing over and over . . .*

41 INT. DAVID'S BEDROOM. NIGHT.

DAVID *is asleep. A shadow falls across him. It's* PETER. *He comes over and stands there, burdened, watching over his sleeping son. He kisses* DAVID *lovingly on the forehead.*

42 INT. AUSTRALIA-SOVIET SOCIETY. MEETING ROOM. NIGHT.

DAVID *bows to warm applause.*

SECRETARY: Thank you Comrade Helfgott; your son is a
     credit to you.

PETER *proudly puts his hand on* DAVID's *shoulder. On the wall there's a communist flag and a Stalin portrait.*

The gathering consists of 25 people, members of the society. One woman, in her mid-seventies, warmly applauds her appreciation of DAVID's *talent.*

Cut to later. Cocktails are being served. PETER *is involved in a discussion. He looks around for* DAVID. *No sign.*

43 THE SOCIETY READING ROOM. NIGHT.

DAVID *takes a book from the shelf – it's on Russia. A* GIRL, *about 17, stares at him through the shelves.*

GIRL: You play beautifully.

DAVID: Thank you.

GIRL: My name is Sonia.

DAVID: I'm David.

SONIA: I know who you are.

She laughs; so does DAVID. *He's quite taken.*

SONIA: You have the most wonderful hands.

He looks at his hands, like he'd never noticed. Then looks at hers.

DAVID: So do you.

She smiles warmly.

SONIA: You're going to America?

DAVID: That's right.

SONIA: Perhaps one day you will go to Russia too.

DAVID: Yes. Why not?

PETER (O/S): David.

DAVID *puts his hands in his pockets.*

DAVID: Right here.

PETER *gives* SONIA *a charming smile.*

33

PETER: Excuse us. There is someone important who wants to meet you, David.

44 THE SOCIETY MEETING ROOM. NIGHT.

We recognise the old woman from above – KATHERINE SUSANNAH PRICHARD. *Her face reflects a sharp intelligence and strong humanity.*

KATHERINE: I've never met anyone who plays the piano as beautifully as you, David.

DAVID: And I've never met a writer before, Mrs Prichard.

KATHERINE: You must he very proud of him.

PETER: As proud as a father can be.

KATHERINE *smiles.*

KATHERINE: I have a long-suffering old piano at home.

PETER: A suffering piano?

KATHERINE: From neglect. Perhaps you'd come and play it for me, David.

PETER *goes to speak, but* DAVID *interrupts.*

DAVID: Oh yes, anything to help.

KATHERINE: I'd like that very much.

DAVID: Me too.

SECRETARY (O/S): Your attention Comrades. I wish to propose a toast to our founder –

KATHERINE: That's my cue. Excuse me.

SECRETARY: – and very special guest this evening, Katherine Susannah Prichard.

PETER *applauds along with everyone else.*

PETER: You will learn much from this old woman, David. She has been to Soviet Union.

As KATHERINE *joins the* SECRETARY *up front, she smiles at* DAVID.

PETER (*nudges* DAVID): Smile. Look happy.

47 EXT. HELFGOTT HOUSE. DAY.

DAVID *hurries out the front door excitedly at the sound of the* POSTMAN's *whistle. The* POSTMAN *finds a letter for* DAVID *in his satchel and holds it away before playfully dropping it into the letter box.* DAVID *grabs it and registers where it's come from.*

DAVID: America!

48 INT. HELFGOTT HOUSE. NIGHT.

DAVID *excitedly reads a letter from 'The Mickleburg family – New Jersey'.*

DAVID: '. . . we have been informed of your exceptional talent and can only say how privileged we feel to have you come and stay with us'.

PETER *listens as he chops vegetables on a board, alongside several marrow bones.*

DAVID: 'You will be pleased to know that we are having the Bosendorfer tuned especially for you.'

PETER *scoops the vegetables into a steaming pot.*

DAVID: 'We eagerly await your innement – '

MARGARET: Imminent, fool.

SUZIE: I wonder if they've got a cadillac?

DAVID: 'Imminent arrival . . . And look forward to hearing you play for us. Kindest wishes, Simon and Basha Mickleburg.'

PETER *chops more vegetables – the simple words are like daggers.* RACHEL *is mindful of his brooding silence.*

SUZIE: Read it again.

MARGARET: Not again!

She turns the radio up.

DAVID: You're just jealous.

PETER *simmers . . .*

SUZIE: Just the bit about the parakeet and the dog and the two cats.

MARGARET *puts her hands over her ears.*

DAVID: '. . . you'll enjoy the company of our parakeet and our poodle called *Margaret*'.

MARGARET: Pig! It is not!

She grabs the letter and DAVID *tries to get it; all yelling, playing 'keepings off' around the room.*

DAVID: Jealous, jealous, give it!

MARGARET: Pig! Pig!

PETER: ENOUGH!

He sweeps a bottle of milk off the bench; it explodes at SUZIE's *feet.*

PETER: Enough of this nonsense!

DAVID *pales as* PETER *tears the letter up.* SUZIE *cries.*

DAVID: Daddy?

PETER: Forget it! You are not going. David is not going anywhere. (*Silence.*) What are you looking at, you fools? He is not going to America! I won't let anyone destroy this family!

DAVID: Daddy, but Daddy please –

PETER: I know what is best, David. I know because I am your father and this is your family.

Stunned silence. DAVID *runs out of the house.*

PETER: David! David come back –

The door slams.

RACHEL (*in Yiddish*): Why now!? Why!?

PETER *slaps her.*

49 EXT. BEN ROSEN'S HOUSE. NIGHT.

The house is in darkness. DAVID *knocks. He's been running, in a sweat.*

DAVID: Mr Rosen?

No answer.

DAVID: Mr Rosen. It's David. (*He bangs at the door.*)
    Please Mr Rosen. Please . . .

There's nobody home. DAVID *slides down the door,
clutching his knees, bewildered.*

Cut to water rippling in the moonlight. DAVID's
*reflection appears in the pond. He watches the
distortion of his face in the water, then slaps the surface
and after a moment the image settles again. He puts his
head under, right up to his shoulders.*

Cut to underwater, DAVID's *face, as bubbles escape
from his mouth. In fact we are in:*

50 INT. HELFGOTT BATHROOM. NIGHT.

We realise DAVID's *face is underwater in the bath. He
surfaces, for air . . . and just stares, breathing
awkwardly.*

PETER *enters in a dressing gown.*

PETER: Come on David, you have been long enough. Are
    you feeling better now? Silly boy, all this nonsense.
    This is your home, this is where you belong . . .

DAVID's POV: PETER *peeling off his dressing gown and
singlet, talking but there is no sound – it's like a dream.*
PETER *goes to get in but stops as he sees something in
the bath that horrifies him.*

PETER: David! (*He slaps David's head.*) You animal. You disgusting animal.

He slashes at DAVID *with a white singlet, splashing water everywhere.*

PETER: To shit in the bath. To do this to me. You callous boy. To shit like an animal.

DAVID *barely reacts as the attack with the wet singlet continues, across his bare back, his head . . . water arcs across the small bathroom with each blow.*

Just as suddenly as it started, it's over. PETER *is gone. Water runs down the walls like blood. A drop forms on the flickering light globe, then falls.* DAVID *just stares . . . in shock. Silence.*

51 INT. SYNAGOGUE. DAY.

RACHEL *is huddled with* SUZIE, MARGARET *and* LOUISE *in the upper balcony. The Jewish community watches as* DAVID *sings from the Torah, taking his bar mitzvah, head bowed, almost cowering.*

ROSEN *senses something is wrong. He looks across at* PETER *whose stern unwavering expression gives nothing away.*

Close-up: PETER, *a man of steel.*

53 EXT. HELFGOTT HOUSE. NIGHT.

Wide shot. The house is in near darkness. ROSEN *walks up purposefully and scrapes the front gate open. He knocks at the door. No answer.*

54 INT. HELFGOTT HOUSE. NIGHT.

In the hallway – ROSEN's *silhouette through the opaque glass. He knocks again.*

Reveal PETER, *in the shadowy darkness, the outside world completely shut out.*

54a INT. THE LOUNGEROOM. NIGHT.

The air is thick with tension. RACHEL *amuses little* LOUISE. SUZIE *flips through the scrapbook.* MARGARET *fingers the same note on the piano. All stop as the knocking echoes again through the solemn quiet, like a knell. Silence.*

MARGARET: This house is like a concentration camp.

She lets the piano lid drop shut. In the hallway ROSEN's *shadow waits at the door.*

ROSEN (V/O): Peter? I know you can hear me. Don't do this to David. You mustn't.

PETER's *eyes glow with anger in the darkness.*

Silence.

55 EXT. HELFGOTT HOUSE. NIGHT.

ROSEN: Peter!

ROSEN *gives up, turns to go, but then as an afterthought*:

ROSEN: Whatever you do, don't inflict bloody
    Rachmaninov on him. He's not ready!

56 INT. HELFGOTT HOUSE. NIGHT.

In the hallway – ROSEN's *shadow disappears. The gate
is heard scraping open as he leaves.*

PETER *just stands there. The sound of* ROSEN's *car is
heard driving away, the headlights flicker across* PETER's
face.

57 INT. HELFGOTT HOUSE. NIGHT.

PETER *stands over the bed where* DAVID *lies, facing
away.*

PETER: David . . . (*No reply.*) David. My boy? Still you
    don't speak to me?

Pause.

PETER: It's a terrible thing to hate, to hate your father.

Silence. He sits on the bed.

PETER: Life is cruel, but music, it will always be your
    friend. Everything else will let you down in the end.

Everything. Believe me. (*Pause.*) Please don't hate me. David.

He begins to cry. He sobs . . .

DAVID *looks at his father crying, full of confusion. Their eyes meet and* PETER *pulls* DAVID *up and hugs him.* DAVID *throws his arms around his neck.*

PETER (*in Yiddish*): Don't hate me.

PETER *kisses* DAVID *repeatedly on the side of the face, all the while stuttering:*

PETER: It's tough, life can be tough but you have to survive, say it. You have to –

DAVID: Survive, Daddy . . .

PETER: That's right, David. No one will love you like me. You can't trust anyone but I will always be there . . . always be with you, forever. Do you understand?

DAVID: Yes, Daddy, forever . . .

They hug as we begin to pull back . . . looking down on them.

PETER: Forever and ever . . .

PETER AND DAVID: Forever and ever . . .

58 INT. DAVID'S ROOM. EDEN LODGE. NIGHT.

ADULT DAVID *sits on the floor in the middle of the room, scrounging for a match amidst the mess of paper and music spread around him. He picks up something.*

*It's a crumpled old letter with distinctive letterhead:
Royal College of Music.* DAVID *peers myopically at it –
we only glimpse a few words: 'Dear Mr Helfgott, we
are pleased to inform you . . .'*

*Fade up – music, from the past – 'Sospiro' by Liszt. It
continues over:*

59 INT. TRAIN TUNNEL. DAY. THE PAST.

The train exits a tunnel into bright strobing light.

61 EXT. OVERGROWN DRIVEWAY OF KATHERINE'S HOUSE.
AFTERNOON.

*Bright light pours through a jungle of trees and exotic
plants.* DAVID *makes his way down the long overgrown
drive. Finally, a small weatherboard cottage comes into
view, its verandah wreathed in wisteria, jasmine and
honeysuckle.*

62 EXT. KATHERINE'S HOUSE. VERANDAH. NIGHT.

A photograph of DAVID *is removed from a paper bag.
It's* DAVID *at his best, supremely confident.*

KATHERINE: Perfect; I'll treasure it until the day I die.

DAVID *has finished eating dinner.*

KATHERINE: Are you full?

DAVID: Full as a goog, Katherine; full as a goog.

63 INT. KATHERINE'S HOUSE. NIGHT.

DAVID *plays the final bars of the Appassionata. When he finishes, he looks to* KATHERINE *in front of several photos on the mantel, lost in the past, moved by his playing.*

KATHERINE: Each time you play 'Sospiro' it expresses so completely . . . the inexpressible.

DAVID: Is that good?

KATHERINE (*sits next to him*): It's divine.

DAVID: Inexpressibly divine.

KATHERINE: Quite!

He starts playing again.

DAVID: Tell me a story, Katherine. What story is it today?

DAVID *watches her – eyes closed, head swaying.*

KATHERINE: A new story – drops of water.

DAVID: Raindrops?

KATHERINE: Yes, raindrops.

DAVID'*s head sways as he plays the passage.*

KATHERINE: Listen. It's the wind.

Cut to the verandah. Moonlight filters through.

DAVID (V/O): The wind!

Leaves flutter across the ground . . . Branches sway . . .

DAVID (V/O): The stream . . .

KATHERINE (V/O): The river . . .

DAVID (V/O): The ocean, Katherine!

65 INT. KATHERINE'S HOUSE. DAY.

The photograph of DAVID, *now framed, is on the mantel.*

KATHERINE'S VOICE: . . . You are Krishna, Christ and Dionysus. In your beauty, tenderness and strength . . .

The camera moves towards the piano, where DAVID *is stooped over. We just see the top of his head until he looks up and, we realise, years have passed.*

DAVID *is now a young adult. He scribbles the words of the poem onto a score, awed by their beauty as she continues to read.*

KATHERINE: 'To you, all these wild weeds and wind flowers of my life. I bring my lord and lay them at your feet.'

66 EXT. KATHERINE'S HOUSE. NIGHT.

Wide shot. Lights burn warmly in the windows of the old home. Cut to: the front door opens and KATHERINE *sees* DAVID *out.*

DAVID: Good night, Katherine.

She kisses him warmly. He ambles off, awkward as a puppy, into the night.

KATHERINE: Good luck, David.

67 INT. CONCERT HALL. NIGHT.

Stagehands carefully position the grand piano onstage. Lights and curtains are being set for a performance. Cut to backstage, hands soak in a steaming bowl of water, next to it is a score of Rachmaninov's Third. DAVID *warms his hands in the water, the poise and confidence of his younger years gone, replaced by a shambling insecurity. He throws a nervous look around at the other contestants:*

A CELLIST *warms up, a* VIOLINIST *paces, a* CONTESTANT *goes over her score while another pianist,* ROGER, 25, *warms up on an old upright piano in the corner.*

Cut to the foyer. The audience assembles, waiting to go in. A poster tells us the occasion is the 'ABC – NATIONAL CONCERTO COMPETITION'.

Arriving amidst the furs and jewellery, PETER *is just another face in the crowd. Something draws his attention:* BEN ROSEN *on the stair. He catches* PETER *looking. Neither hides their contempt.* ROSEN *comments to his companion:*

ROSEN: Poor man's Leopold Mozart.

Cut to onstage. A piano cover is removed revealing gold letters: 'BOSENDORFER'. DAVID *is drawn towards the*

49

grand piano, mesmerised by its magnificence. He circles it, oblivious to everything else. The sound of applause fades up . . .

ANNOUNCER (V/O): That was our final contestant –

72 INT. KATHERINE'S HOUSE. NIGHT.

ANNOUNCER (*radio V/O, continued*): . . . *David Helfgott, who gave a stirring performance of Rachmaninov's Third Concerto for Piano in D Minor . . .*

KATHERINE *looks at the framed photo of adolescent* DAVID.

KATHERINE: Bravo, David.

ANNOUNCER (*radio* V/O): The judges will now confer.

73 INT. CONCERT HALL. NIGHT.

In the audience, PETER *is anxious as the jury confers.* ROSEN *observes him. Backstage,* THE CONTESTANTS *assemble in readiness, wishing each other luck.*

An envelope is handed to the ANNOUNCER *who adjusts his bow-tie then steps onto the stage.* DAVID *shuffles nervously on the spot, standing next to* ROGER, *whose focus is on the stage.*

DAVID: It's a tough game isn't it, Roger?

ROGER: A bloodsport.

ANNOUNCER: Ladies and gentlemen.

PETER *leans forward in anticipation.*

ANNOUNCER: I am pleased to announce the winner of this year's ABC National Concerto Competition is – Roger Woodward.

Applause. PETER's *face turns to stone.*

DAVID: Well done, well done, Roger.

The other contestants congratulate ROGER *then he walks out onto the stage to a loud ovation.*

DAVID *watches from the wings as* ROGER *takes his bows in the bright spotlight.*

75 INT. KATHERINE'S HOUSE. DAY.

A framed photo of KATHERINE's *father is on the mantel, amidst others including the one of* DAVID *as a bright adolescent.*

DAVID: What was he like, Katherine?

She looks up from her book.

Your father.

She puts the book aside.

KATHERINE: He was forever busy in his study. 'Go away, Kattie, I'm writing,' he'd always say. One day, I was very young, I got so annoyed I emptied the inkpots all over his desk and I scrawled on his work, pages of it. When he saw it he stood there seething with anger; I could feel it.

David fills with dread.

'What are you doing?' he shouted.

It startles DAVID, *feeding his own fears.*

KATHERINE: There was this terrible silence. I just stared at him and said, 'Go away, daddy, I'm writing.'

David is suspended.

He ran at me and picked me up, and cuddled me breathless. My first literary effort he always called it.

Silence. KATHERINE *sees there's something troubling* DAVID.

KATHERINE: What is it? (*No reply.*) David?

He extracts a letter from his pocket. She takes it and reads it.

KATHERINE: The Royal College of Music. A scholarship. David that's marvellous!

DAVID: Won't cuddle me Katherine, oh no.

He wrings his hands full of anxiety.

KATHERINE: He can't stop you, David.

DAVID: Such an angry lion.

KATHERINE: Nonsense, he's a pussycat.

She holds him comfortingly and looks into his uncertain eyes to give him strength.

KATHERINE: I'll miss you.

76 INT. KATHERINE'S HOUSE. DAY.

Close-up – a small box which KATHERINE *takes from the sideboard.*

KATHERINE: These were for my son but he left home before I could give them to him.

DAVID *opens it and takes out an exquisite pair of red fur-lined kid gloves.*

KATHERINE: You'll need them. It gets very, very cold in London.

77 EXT. COUNTRY ROAD. DUSK.

A fiery red sky. DAVID *walks along, churning with anxiety. He stops and takes the gloves out of the gladstone bag he's carrying. He draws them on, then walks off leaving the bag behind.*

78 INT. HELFGOTT HOUSE. NIGHT.

DAVID *enters quietly, makes his way through the darkness.*

PETER'S VOICE: Where have you been?

A table lamp is switched on to reveal PETER *sitting there.*

DAVID: I missed the train.

PETER'*s eyes glow with hostility.*

PETER: That Prichard woman!

DAVID *goes to move away.*

PETER: What is this?

The gloves DAVID'*s wearing. He takes a backward step.*

PETER: What? (*Stands.*) Look at me. Look at me!

DAVID *has no choice.* PETER'*s eyes burn through him.*

PETER: David?

DAVID *slowly extracts the letter, backs away as* PETER *reads.*

PETER: You think you can just do as you please? Huh?

DAVID: I . . . I want to go; I'm going. You can't stop me.

A terrible silence. Then PETER *comes at* DAVID *like a lumbering bear.*

PETER: I am your father. Your father! Who has done everything for you; you cruel, callous boy!

DAVID *tries uselessly to fend him off.*

DAVID: Daddy –

PETER: I am your father!

He slaps DAVID *around the head, knocking his glasses off.*

DAVID: Please Daddy –

PETER: Stupid boy!

SUZIE *runs in and tries to pull* PETER *away.*

SUZIE: No –

PETER *gives* SUZIE *a backhand.*

DAVID: It's not Suzie's fault.

DAVID *charges forward, crashing* PETER *into the wall.*

RACHEL (*racing in*): Stop it! Stop it!

PETER *throws* DAVID *across the room.* MARGARET
intervenes.

PETER: Get out of the way!

He picks up a chair and throws it against the wall.

79 EXT. HELFGOTT HOUSE. NIGHT.

RACHEL (V/O) (*screams*): No!

Dogs bark. Neighbours' lights go on.

80 INT. HELFGOTT HOUSE. NIGHT.

PETER: You want to go? Go! Go on!

He has DAVID *in a headlock, choking him. They bang
into the walls, locked together in a fierce struggle. The
photo of the rabbi crashes to the ground. Furniture is
skittled – chess pieces scattered.*

RACHEL (*screams, in Yiddish*): No! Stop! Stop!

*She bashes his arms with her fists trying to get him to
let go of* DAVID *who can't breathe.* MARGARET *tries to
pull* PETER *away.*

MARGARET: I'll get the police!

Finally, PETER *lets go of* DAVID *who slumps to the floor.*

PETER: He's alright, leave him.

Catching his breath, he sees his terrified family, only now registering the horror of what has happened.

Silence. DAVID *fumbles for his glasses. He picks up the crumpled letter.*

PETER: David, are you alright? Are you?

PETER *approaches, with remorse.*

PETER: Come on, David.

DAVID: I'm old enough to make up my own mind.

He backs away, into the corridor.

PETER (*laughs*): He thinks he's going to London.

DAVID: I've been accepted by the Royal College of Music.

DAVID *is full of confusion.*

PETER: What do you think is going to happen to you in London?

DAVID *wipes his bloody nose, edges down the corridor.*

PETER: David, listen to me. If you go, you will never come back into this house again. You will never be anybody's son, the girls will lose a brother. Is that what you want? You want to destroy this family.

DAVID: I'm sorry, sorry –

He opens the door. RACHEL *holds the girls, all crying.*

PETER: If you love me you will stop this nonsense; you
  will not step outside that door. Don't make me do it!

DAVID: . . . Sorry . . .

PETER: David!

DAVID *steps over the threshold.*

PETER: You will be punished for the rest of your life!!

SUZIE: DAVID!

The door slams shut.

81 EXT. COUNTRY ROAD. NIGHT.

DAVID *runs, in a sweat, on the road to* KATHERINE's.
*The headlights of a car bear straight down on him. It
blasts its horn as it swerves around him.*

Cut to a blazing fire in:

82 EXT. HELFGOTT BACKYARD. NIGHT.

Music scores burn, school books, David's clothes . . .
PETER *throws another pile on, stokes the flames.*

Burning in the fire is the scrapbook – images of YOUNG
DAVID *surrender to the flames.*

83 EXT. LONDON. DAY.

'The Royal College of Music' – *gold letters carved in stone above the entrance.* ADULT DAVID *looks up: we are back in the present. He absorbs the imposing building as he shuffles up the steps. Behind him, the magnificent dome of the Albert Hall.*

On the kerb, GILLIAN *is getting out of a taxi. When she looks around, there's no sign of* DAVID.

84 INT. RCOM CORRIDOR. DAY. THE PRESENT.

DAVID *shuffles along, past the practice rooms from where different instruments sound, merging into one another as* DAVID *continues on his journey, his face full of childish wonder. He hears something distinct . . . a piano. He goes to the source, a practice room at the end of the corridor. He peers through the narrow glass panel, into:*

85 INT. PRACTICE ROOM. DAY. THE PRESENT.

There's a female student practising with her teacher. She notices the face at the door a moment before it ducks out of sight.

DAVID *sneaks another impish look in . . . then quickly retreats. Again, his face slides into frame and retreats.*

As if by magic, when the face appears again, it's no longer ADULT DAVID, *but the* YOUNGER DAVID, *longer hair falling in ringlets around his face.*

86 INT. PRACTICE ROOM. DAY.

We are back in the past and there's an elderly teacher in the practice room who looks at his watch impatiently to make a point.

PARKES: Bravo, David. Now remind me why I'm here.

DAVID (*enters*): Sorry, Mr Parkes, sorry.

PROFESSOR CECIL PARKES *is in his sixties. His left arm hangs limply by his side, crippled by a stroke.*

PARKES: It's fortunate I'm a deeply forgiving human being.

DAVID'S VOICE: Liszt was like that, wasn't he, a great humanitarian – not that I ever met him, knew him personally or anything but he had a respect for every living breathing creature; so that was nice of him, wasn't it? Or so I read. (*Plonks a book down.*)

Very improvisatorial, very sensual, Mr Parkes. Virtuosic!

PARKES: Bacchanalian! Boldness of attack!

He bashes out chords with his one good arm.

PARKES: Diablerie! The Devil, David!

DAVID: Whooaah, mustn't break the piano.

PARKES: Liszt broke plenty!

DAVID: Right!

Swept up, DAVID *bashes out some chords –* PARKES *stops him.*

PARKES (*quietly*): But you must play what's on the page; you're not Liszt, remember.

DAVID: Not even slightly Mozart.

PARKES *plays (with his good hand) to demonstrate.*

PARKES: Come on, fill in for this useless arm of mine.

David plays the 'other hand'.

The notes first, your interpretation comes on top of them.

DAVID: On top, yes.

PARKES *enjoys their playing together. He likes* DAVID.

PARKES: You agree, do you?

DAVID: Oh yes, I always agree.

PARKES: Is that wise?

DAVID: I don't know. Is it?

They play on. DAVID *works the pedals; he's wearing odd shoes, a black one and a brown one.*

PARKES: Don't forget, it's on the page.

DAVID: Well yes, the notes are, but not the feeling, the emotion which is what I feel.

PARKES: You mustn't sacrifice everything to emotion. It's a question of balance.

DAVID: Is that the question, Professor?

PARKES: Precisely.

DAVID: I thought so.

87 INT. RCOM FOYER. DAY.

A throng of students is going up the stairs. DAVID *is coming down the other way, bumping into everyone.*

DAVID: Sorry sorry, oops, beg pardon. Sorry, I'll stand still. There!

STUDENT: Bravo, David.

DAVID: Whooahhh, bravo bravo Sarah. You look lovely today, Sarah, simply beautiful.

SARAH: Thank you, David.

DAVID: You too, Muriel.

MALE STUDENT: Ease up, Helfgott.

Laughter; DAVID*'s popular with them.*

REGISTRAR: Mr Helfgott. Your allowance cheque.

Two students – ASHLEY *and* ROBERT *– look on.*

ROBERT (to ASHLEY): Pay day. David!

They flank DAVID *as he heads through the foyer.*

ROBERT: You missed the bank. Pity! You'll have to wait until tomorrow.

DAVID: Can't bank on the bank.

ASHLEY: We know someone who'll cash it, David.

DAVID: Do we Ashley? Do we really?

ROBERT: What are friends for?

As they exit to:

88 EXT. RCOM. DAY.

DAVID: 'All you need is friends', whoahhh. It's what The Beatles say.

ASHLEY: 'Love' dear David . . .

DAVID: Yes, Ashley darling?

ROBERT: Taxi!

89 INT. SOHO STRIP CLUB. NIGHT.

DAVID *crosses to* ASHLEY *and* ROBERT *with a tray full of drinks, while a stripper bumps and grinds. They drink at* DAVID's *expense and puff on cigars, including* DAVID.

90 EXT. SOHO. NIGHT.

DAVID *walks along stuffing his mouth with chocolate and Coke, taking in the sights. A transvestite with bright red-dyed hair and make-up steps out of a doorway –* RAY.

RAY: Got a cigarette, love?

DAVID: A cigarette love – love a cigarette.

He offers the packet.

RAY: I'm Ray.

DAVID: Ray? Ray! Raylene! Whooah, pleased to meet you. I'm David, David Helfgott. Ridiculous!

RAY *lights up the cigarette, then puts an arm around* DAVID.

RAY: You're very friendly, aren't you David?

DAVID: Friendly? Do you think so? That's very important isn't it?

RAY: If you say so, sweetheart.

He steers innocent DAVID *into an alleyway.*

91 EXT. TRAFALGAR SQUARE. SUNRISE.

Close-up: the bobbing face of a pigeon. It coos. DAVID's *eyes blink open. He sees the pigeon and coos back. His face has traces of make-up on it. Under his jacket he's now wearing the lurex vest we saw on* RAY.

New angle. DAVID *is curled up under a massive statue of a lion (which guards Nelson's column). Nearby a* MAN *hoses away birdshit.*

Wide shot. DAVID *shuffles off in the early morning light, across the empty square.*

93 INT/EXT. UPPER WINDOW. RCOM. DAY.

PARKES *and another teacher,* GORDON VINEY, *50, sip tea as they look out the window onto the street below.*

PARKES: He has the most fantastic hands.

VINEY: Not connected to anything above the shoulders.

94 THEIR POV.

DAVID *hurrying up some steps in the College grounds. He drops music everywhere.*

PARKES: He's a little fragile.

VINEY: A chopinzee!

PARKES *isn't amused.*

PARKES: I've seen enough to suggest he can make the finals of the concerto trials.

VINEY: And what have you seen, Cecil?

A gleam in PARKES' *eye.*

PARKES: Moments of genius.

VINEY (*laugh, bemused*): Genius. Oh really!

POV below – DAVID *scrambles chaotically after his music.*

95 INT. RCOM. DAY.

DAVID *hurries down the corridor.*

VOICE: David!

He spins around to be met by GILLIAN *walking towards*

him – we are back in the present. ADULT DAVID *looks completely baffled.*

ADULT DAVID: Gillian, what are you doing here?

96 INT. DIRECTOR'S OFFICE. DAY. PRESENT.

RONALD IRWIN *– the Director of the College – is a distinguished-looking forty. He pours tea for* GILLIAN *while* DAVID *looks at framed photos and various certificates on the wall, shuffling from one frame to another.*

IRWIN: Is he aware of what happened? Does he remember?

GILLIAN: Ask him.

IRWIN: Do you remember much from your student days, David?

DAVID: Oh yes, yes absolutely. Everything. Well kind of, kind of; or is it a bit of a blank, a bit of a scrabble, the pieces missing – is that it?

GILLIAN: You're the only one that knows that.

DAVID: That's right darling, the only one –

GILLIAN: You were here.

DAVID: I was, I was here, that's right I was; it seems to be true. Is it true? Or is that just the way it is?

GILLIAN: The way what is, David?

DAVID: Scrabble, darling. (*To Irwin.*) It's a tough game, isn't it? A bloodsport.

GILLIAN: Not quite.

He mumbles on as he turns back to the photos.

GILLIAN: Filling in the blanks is what it's all about, as you can see.

IRWIN *takes in the mumbling, stooping figure of* DAVID, *finding it hard to believe.*

IRWIN: That performance he gave for the concerto finals, Rachmaninov's Third. I'll never forget it; I doubt anyone could.

DAVID: Whooaahh Professor!

It's a photo of PARKES – *now Sir Cecil Parkes.*

97 INT. RCOM CORRIDOR. DAY.

Doors burst open and YOUNG DAVID *tears down the corridor. We are back in the past. He slides to a stop in front of a notice: 'CONCERTO MEDAL FINALISTS (Patron: H.M. The Queen Mother)'.*

'David Helfgott' is on the list of six pinned on the notice board.

ROBERT: How on earth did we manage to make the finals, dear David?

DAVID – *out of breath – can't believe it.*

ASHLEY: You're a conductor's nightmare.

DAVID *pulls a 'nightmare' face as he registers his name on the list.*

DAVID: It's true, it's true.

ROBERT: What are we going to do?

DAVID: We're going to win, Ashley-Robert. We're going to win!

98 INT. PRACTICE ROOM. DAY.

PARKES: Are you sure?

He takes the Rachmaninov Concerto score from DAVID.

DAVID: I'm never sure about anything, Mr Parkes.

PARKES: The Rach' 3? It's monumental.

DAVID: A mountain! The hardest piece you could everest play.

A moment. PARKES *dares to even consider it.*

PARKES: No one's ever been mad enough to attempt the Rach' 3.

DAVID: Am I mad enough Professor? Am I?

99 INT. RCOM CORRIDOR. DAY. THE PRESENT.

STUDENTS *mill past* ADULT DAVID, GILLIAN *and the College* DIRECTOR *walking in the opposite direction.*

DAVID'S VOICE: 'The point is, I didn't come to London to enjoy myself, got to concentrate . . .'

100 INT. RCOM. SAME CORRIDOR. DAY. THE PAST.

STUDENTS *clear a path for* YOUNG DAVID, *bumping past them, in a flap.*

DAVID'S VOICE: 'Got to practise, Katherine; there's three important things Mr Parkes says: "work, work, work" . . .'

DAVID *hurries from one door to the next, looking into the practice rooms which are all occupied by students practising on the pianos . . . room after room.*

DAVID'S VOICE: 'You see, I am to play in a very special competition and the winner gets to play at the Albert Hall before her Highest Royalness the Queen Mum . . .'

He arrives at a practice room door, the glass obscured by a jacket hanging on the inside. He opens the door and is set back by the sight of TWO STUDENTS *in an embrace.*

DAVID: Whooahh, a duet! Sorry.

He shuts the door, sits in the corridor and proceeds to practise in his head.

101 INT/EXT. PIANO STORE. DAY.

DAVID'S VOICE: 'So I bought a piano, how's that Katherine? . . .'

DAVID *presses his face against the window, looking in at the exquisite range of grand and concert pianos.*

71

102 INT. KATHERINE'S HOUSE. DAY.

KATHERINE *smiles, standing at the mantel, listening to a reel to reel tape recorder in motion . . .*

DAVID'S VOICE: '. . . a truly beautiful piano . . .'

103 INT. DAVID'S BEDSIT. DAY.

DAVID'S VOICE: 'A suffering piano, like yours . . .'

The piano is a horrible hand-painted white, adorned with psychedelic flowers – a '5 Pound Special' (scrawled on the front). DAVID *is seated on the floor of the grotty basement room, a tangle of books, music, clothes, Coke bottles and chocolate wrappers. He chews chocolate as he talks into the microphone of a reel to reel tape machine . . .*

DAVID'S VOICE: 'Got a letter from Daddy, well kind of, because I wrote it you see and he sent it back. Ah well, it's very hard, to express . . . the inexpressible, Katherine . . .'

DAVID *stops the tape. Pinned on the wall is the photo of adolescent* DAVID *with* PETER *and numerous envelopes (addressed to* PETER *in* DAVID'*s scrawl) all marked: 'Return to Sender'.*

DAVID: Ah well . . .

He stares, takes a tablet from one of many bottles on the piano.

104 INT. PRACTICE ROOM. DAY. BEGIN MONTAGE.

The camera circles PARKES *as he rounds on* DAVID *playing rapid exercises on the piano.*

PARKES: Performing's a risk, there's no safety net. And people come to see you fall. Arpeggios, first inversion! (DAVID *obeys.*) Make no mistake David – it's dangerous, people get hurt!

DAVID *practises as if his life depended on it.*

105 INT. DAVID'S BEDSIT. NIGHT.

DAVID *crouches, his face an inch from the floor, his fingers performing a spidery exercise as he lifts them up and down on the threadbare carpet, getting faster and faster until you can barely see them.*

106 INT. PRACTICE ROOM. DAY.

PARKES: B major scale at 180 beats a minute. (DAVID *takes a breath.*) Contrary motion . . . Come on, David. Endure!

DAVID'*s hands are a blur . . .*

A series of shots as DAVID *progresses from one exercise to the next,* PARKES *barking different instructions* ('Melodic Minor' . . . 'Harmonic Minor', *etc).*

PARKES: Think of it as two separate melodies, jousting for supremacy. Your hands, giants, with ten fingers each.

DAVID *flails at the keyboard.*

PARKES: F sharp major scales in thirds! (*Sotto voce.*) That's a bitch.

DAVID *punishes the keys, huffing and puffing.*

107 EXT. SOHO. NIGHT.

DAVID *walks along studying the score for the Rach 3. He sees something up ahead which causes him to take cover in a shop doorway.*

New angle. RAY *walks past with a friend.* DAVID *checks the all-clear then continues in the opposite direction.*

108 INT. RCOM LIBRARY. DAY.

PARKES: You have to be able to play it blindfolded.

DAVID: Ooh, that's a trick.

There are dozens of scores and technical books spread out in front of them.

PARKES: Your hands must form the unbreakable habit of playing the notes so you can forget them and let this take over. (*Points to his heart*). That's where it comes from!

109 INT. DAVID'S BEDSIT. NIGHT.

DAVID *practises blindfolded. Seated on the piano is a scrawny cat.*

Later: DAVID *eats from a can of sardines, at the same time handfeeding the cat.*

110 INT. PRACTICE ROOM. DAY.

DAVID *plays the lyrical cadenza from Rach 3.*

PARKES: The page for God's sake! The notes!

DAVID (*stops*): I was forgetting them, Professor.

PARKES: Would it be asking too much to learn them first?

DAVID: And then forget them?

PARKES: Right. (*Slams the lid down.*) Just give me the fingering.

DAVID *fingers the notes on the lid. The cadenza continues into:*

111 INT. DAVID'S BEDSIT. NIGHT.

Shivering DAVID *sizes up one hand wearing the kid gloves and proceeds to cut the finger-tips off, turning the gloves into a pair of mittens. Wearing a greatcoat, he rubs his hands together and practises.*

Headlights outside create weird shadows as DAVID *plays the cadenza softly, softly . . .*

DAVID (*to the cat*): How does that sound?

The photo of PETER *keeps an eye on* DAVID.

112 INT. PRACTICE ROOM. DAY.

Light pours in.

PARKES: We're going to rest muscles and fingers today, David and give the imagination a workout. Second movement – Intermezzo. Oboe!

He sings the accompaniment. DAVID *catches on and sings the piano part with feeling.*

113 INT. RCOM. DAY.

DAVID *and* PARKES *walk downstairs, along the corridor singing the concerto with gusto, completely immersed in their performances. They stop, face to face, for a lively duet; students mill past.*

DAVID *and* PARKES *burst through a door as they build to a climax, filling the foyer with the joy of the music.*

114 EXT. RCOM. DAY.

VINEY's POV *from an above window:*

DAVID *and* PARKES, *arms flailing as they continue their performance up the steps of the Albert Hall.*

VINEY (*grimacing*): Loonies.

115 INT. PRACTICE ROOM. DAY.

DAVID *unleashes an awesome run of chords.*

PARKES: Don't you just love those big fat chords!

DAVID *thrashes the keys.*

PARKES: You have to tame the piano, David, or it'll get away from you; make it do things it's never done. It's a monster; tame it, or it'll swallow you whole.

DAVID *hears it roar, plays possessed, stabbing at the pedals, lashing the keys relentlessly. A clamorous twang stops him.*

Inside the piano the broken string bobs up and down; PARKES *and* DAVID *peer in at it.*

PARKES (*a distinct laugh*): Coming along nicely, David.

116 NIGHT.

DAVID *practises still, on his own. Through the window is the Albert Hall, lights shimmering in the cold night air. End montage.*

117 INT. ROOMING HOUSE. DAY.

A pile of mail on the floor. A hand rifles through it – there's a small parcel, addressed to 'David Helfgott'. DAVID *studies it curiously, then notices a woman stopped on the stairs, mouth agape, looking at him. He smiles, walks back to his room. He's completely naked.*

118 INT. DAVID'S ROOM. DAY.

The parcel is unwrapped. A white card falls out. It's

from the 'Estate of Katherine Susannah Prichard'. DAVID
picks it up and reads it to himself.

DAVID: 'Katherine Susannah Prichard requested that all
personal belongings and remembrances be returned
after her death. Yours . . .'

DAVID *is uncomprehending. He opens The parcel, takes
out several audio tapes and then a picture frame. It's the
photo he gave Katherine. He looks at himself as a
smiling adolescent, through the cracked glass of the
frame, his face reflected in it.*

Dissolve to ADULT DAVID's *face in:*

119 INT. RCOM ARCHIVES. DAY. THE PRESENT.

ADULT DAVID *looks out the window of the archives,
mumbling to himself.*

DAVID: She died, went away, just like that.

GILLIAN: It was years ago.

DAVID: Of course, absolute ages, aeons ago.

GILLIAN: Katherine was very old.

DAVID: Ah well, what can you expect when you're as old
as the hills?

In the background, an ASSISTANT *rummaging up a
ladder hands an archive box to the* DIRECTOR.

DIRECTOR: Here we are, the programmes for the concerto
finals going way back.

GILLIAN *joins him to look over them.* DAVID *smiles at something he's seen out the window.*

DAVID*'s* POV – *below (intercut):*

120 EXT. RCOM/POV. DAY.

The steps leading from the Royal Albert Hall. DAVID *screws his eyes up against the glare of light coming through the window of the archives.*

Below, a MAN *in a long coat, carrying an umbrella, descends the steps.*

121 EXT. RCOM. EARLY MORNING. THE PAST.

We follow the familiar stride across the street to the college. It's PARKES. *He stops by the college entrance, at the familiar pair of red mittens.*

PARKES: David? How long have you been here?

YOUNG DAVID *is sitting there, blue with cold, mittens on.*

DAVID: Mr Parkes, gee . . . I don't know – all night I think. How does that sound?

PARKES: You're frozen. Can't afford for you to get ill now, David.

DAVID: Not now or never, or is the damage done?

PARKES: Damage?

DAVID: That's right. Inside, kind of. Or was I born damaged – like you?

PARKES: I wasn't born like this. (*Looks at his arm.*) It was a stroke.

DAVID: A stroke of bad luck. Whooahhh! Sorry sorry. Sad isn't it?

PARKES *looks genuinely concerned. He sits next to* DAVID.

PARKES: What on earth is the problem?

DAVID: Um . . . well perhaps, you know, if I played well, I could be forgiven.

PARKES: What did you do wrong?

DAVID: Maybe . . . I destroyed the family, David the destroyer.

PARKES: You what?

DAVID: If you do something wrong can you be punished for the rest of your life?

PARKES: David, David –

DAVID: Professor, professor –

PARKES: David, listen to me!

DAVID: Yes Daddy, sorry. Mustn't make you angry, not another angry lion.

PARKES: I'm not your Daddy and I'm not an angry lion.

DAVID: A hyena, more like.

PARKES: A hyena?

DAVID: They sound like . . . (*Imitates* PARKES' *laugh*.) . . . and they don't really hunt, not really – they eat what's left after lions have finished; the leftovers, that's their specialty – leftover soup of the day. Whooahhh.

Pause. PARKES *imitates his own laugh, considers it.*

PARKES: Fascinating.

DAVID: It is, isn't it?

VINEY *walks past – with a snigger at the sight of the two of them seated on the steps.*

VINEY: Morning, Cecil.

PARKES *barely acknowledges* VINEY, *just hisses.*

PARKES: Blithering idiot.

DAVID: I am, I am! It's true, Cecil.

PARKES: Enough woolly thinking. Up! Get up! Follow me.

122 INT. RCOM. NARROW STONE STAIRWAY. NIGHT.

DAVID *follows* PARKES. *Behind a steel grid, in a wall recess is a bust of a frowning Beethoven.*

PARKES: Now he was damaged, deaf as a post.

DAVID: Ooooh, an angry Ludwig . . .

PARKES: Eighth auditory nerve as a matter of fact.

They continue up the narrow stairway, into darkness.

Cut to black. Then a light is switched on.

123 INT. ROOM. PORTRAIT ROOM. NIGHT.

DAVID *takes in the room. A clutter of books and chests, busts, casts and portraits staring at* DAVID. PARKES *shows him a death mask.*

PARKES: Liszt. Warts and all. He was dead when they did that.

DAVID: Dead as a post, poor Franz.

PARKES: You can still pick them up on the Left Bank, quite cheap.

Cut to a cast of a hand being unwrapped from some cloth.

PARKES: Chopin. Look at that wild finger; seems to have been free all its life.

DAVID *absorbs the perfect, white hand.*

PARKES: I've got Rachmaninov in here somewhere.

DAVID: Sergei himself?

PARKES: Not quite.

DAVID *looks around the cramped room, at the portraits and masks.*

PARKES: Here.

A wooden case. Inside is the cast of a hand, exquisitely proportioned, with elegantly long fingers.

PARKES: Magnificent fingers, so virile.

DAVID *extends his hand next to the cast. The similarity is astonishing.*

PARKES: But they don't make the music; they're just electrified little slaves. They do as they're told. (DAVID *flutters his fingers*). Precisely. He heard me play the Rach three.

DAVID: Really?

PARKES: He said he could hear himself in my playing; he said it was as if I had touched his soul. That wasn't too bad was it?

DAVID: Not too bad at all.

DAVID *watches entranced as* PARKES *replaces the cast with reverence. He turns to* DAVID.

PARKES: Now it's your turn, David. Once you've done it, no one can ever take it away from you. (*A lingering moment.*)

And you must play as if there is no tomorrow.

124 INT. RCOM CONCERT HALL. DAY. THE PRESENT.

Light pours into the empty auditorium. GILLIAN *follows the* DIRECTOR *in.* ADULT DAVID *shuffles his way towards the stage.* GILLIAN *takes in the grand old hall. Onstage,*

the Steinway is being tuned. DAVID *steps onto the stage and looks out into the empty auditorium where a cleaner is dusting.* DAVID *stands there . . . a memory stirring to life . . .*

The sound of applause fades in. Reveal the auditorium, now full, brimming with life, the smiling faces of students applauding.

125 THE PAST. NIGHT.

As YOUNG DAVID *takes to the stage for the concerto final, beaming a smile:*

DAVID: Whoaahhh!

The packed audience – of staff and students – applauds his entrance, including PARKES.

PARKES (*to himself*): Come on David, don't let me down.

Full of nerves, DAVID *swings his arms as he ambles towards the grand piano, his awkwardness drawing laughter. So he shoves his hands in his jacket pockets . . . and finds a cigar stub. More laughter as he touches it to his mouth for the benefit of* ASHLEY *and* ROBERT, *hooting in the front row.*

PARKES *grimaces, caught out as* VINEY *leans across.*

VINEY: How many moments of genius today, Cecil?

PARKES *ignores him. Silence falls as* DAVID *sits at the concert grand. He settles, nods to the conductor who*

counts the orchestra into the haunting opening of the
Rach' 3.

DAVID's *foot presses down on the pedal. His hands*
descend on the keys for the first notes. The atmosphere
is heightened, as if a spell has been cast. It flows over
the audience.

126 IN THE BIO BOX.

A student checks the level as the tape rotates on the reel
to reel.

127 INT. CONCERT HALL. DAY.

DAVID *plays with a spellbinding intensity, sucking in air*
to fill his lungs.

Cut to tape recorder reels turning. We are now in:

128 INT. HELFGOTT HOUSE. NIGHT.

PETER *listens to the tape. The tape box is in his hands.*
Scrawled on it is: 'Me playing the Rach 3.' PETER *is*
mesmerised.

129 INT. CONCERT HALL. DAY.

We watch the orchestra as the tempo builds. DAVID's
hands glide through the most difficult sequences. PARKES
sits forward, his good hand willing DAVID *on.*

VINEY *is amazed.*

Close-up on DAVID. *He doesn't hear music, he hears sounds . . . the noise of the other instruments. It's a weird, nerve-shredding cacophony.*

Sweat drips off him onto the keyboard. The silence is surreal, heightened slo-motion as DAVID *endures the pain and the anguish in his body, his hands descending onto the keys, his feet pressing the pedals . . . sounds like deep rumbling explosions . . .*

The audience is caught up in the spell.

All DAVID *hears is a thudding, clattering sound – the hammers inside the piano which is taking on a life of its own, like a mechanical beast he has to subdue before it swallows him up. The percussive sounds of the hammers and the groaning of the piano under assault are deafening.* DAVID *tries to block them out as he plays on . . .*

Resume sound: the music is divine, the audience entranced as they watch DAVID *pour his whole being into it. And as it builds to the finale, the camera swirls around* DAVID *dizzyingly.*

130 INTERCUT. PETER LISTENING TO THE TAPE.

In his hand a gold medal on a ribbon – the Concerto Medal. The agony and awe tell in his face.

131 RESUME. DAVID.

As the concerto climaxes spectacularly, PARKES *leaps to his feet with the rest of the audience, all applauding wildly.*

DAVID: Whooahhh!

He's dripping with sweat . . . it takes moments to realise it's over.

PARKES *slaps his one good arm against his thigh and stabs a triumphant look at* VINEY.

PARKES: *That's* what I call genius.

DAVID *stands, holds his hands up to his sweaty face as the applause deafens. He sweats, hyperventilating.*

DAVID (*mumbling*): Did my best, Daddy . . .

The bright glare of lights swirls. DAVID *gasps short breaths.*

DAVID: How's that . . .

All sound fades out. From DAVID's POV, *it's like a dream, a blur of light and faces. He begins to fall backwards – in slow motion, in silence until his head hits the stage. His spectacles fly off. Eyes wide open, he stares at the bright swirling lights. Silence. Then, a phone rings and rings and rings on.*

Cut to overhead lights in:

132 INT. HOSPITAL WARD. DAY.

DAVID's *glasses are put on a metal tray. Electrodes are placed on his temples. The ECT dial is turned up.*

DAVID's *fingers flutter as the current runs through his body and then they quiver to a stop. He lies there, staring into the void of white light.*

The phone keeps ringing.

Cut to close-up – the phone still ringing. A hand picks up the receiver.

MAN: Hello. (*No response.*) Hello, who is this?

The accent strikes us – it is PETER. *We are in:*

133 INT. HELFGOTT HOUSE. NIGHT

PETER: Hello?

DAVID (V/O): Hello Daddy?

134 INT. PHONE BOOTH. DAY.

DAVID, *hair cut short, pale and gaunt, clutches his bag.*

DAVID: Daddy? I'm back.

135 RESUME – Peter,

numb. He listens in silence, then hangs up slowly. New angle seen through the window; PETER

stands there, stunned. He pulls the blind down. Fade to
black. Slow fade in.

136 EXT. DRIVEWAY. DAY.

A taxi winds its way up the long drive and stops. A
young woman steps out. She walks up some steps, to
the entrance of an imposing old building.

137 INT. PSYCHIATRIC HOSPITAL CORRIDOR. DAY.

Wide shot. The WOMAN *walks down a bare corridor to*
a desk where she exchanges words with a NURSE.

138 EXT. PSYCHIATRIC HOSPITAL GARDENS. DAY.

The WOMAN, *accompanied by the* NURSE, *walks amidst*
several patients enjoying the morning sun. They arrive
at someone seated on a bench.

NURSE: Someone here to see you, David.

No response. SUZIE *walks around to face him.*

SUZIE: It's me, David. Suzie.

We see DAVID's *face for the first time – many years have*
passed. His hair has thinned out – he looks much older
than his early thirties. (This is the DAVID *we recognise*
from scene 2.)

DAVID: Suzie? Suzie! (*Myopic.*) Do we know Suzie?

NURSE: Your sister, David.

DAVID: Sister Nurse, sister Suzie. (*Takes her hand.*) Sweet Suzie, Suzie . . .

Wide shot. The NURSE *leaves.* SUZIE *sits on the bench with* DAVID. DAVID *rocks back and forth, practically oblivious.*

SUZIE: David? I won't be able to come and visit so often.

DAVID: So often, sweet, soft, Suzie.

SUZIE: I'm going to live in Melbourne.

DAVID: Ooh, that's a trick. Don't tell Daddy. The milk, mustn't cry over spilt milk. Ah well, what can you do Margaret?

SUZIE: Margaret's in Israel, remember?

DAVID: I remember Margaret. She called me a pig. All very complicated; complicato in Israel, a battleground. (*Holds his head.*) A war zone, a war; what a bore it's a war . . . a war . . . (*Mumbles on.*)

SUZIE *holds his hand – but he's oblivious to it.*

Cut to branches swaying in the breeze.

Close-up of DAVID, *inanimate, listening to the pure sound of the leaves rustling, tuned right into it. The silence is shattered as a metal trolley crashes into a table. We are not outdoors but in:*

139 INT. PSYCHIATRIC HOSPITAL DAY ROOM. DAY.

DAVID *is seated in front of a window through which we see the swaying branches but the only sound now is the clatter and coldness of the day room where a TV blares high up on a wall and stupefied patients sit slumped in armchairs. A* NURSE *hands him a vial of tablets from the trolley.* DAVID *takes them.*

Close in on DAVID *again – the din fades. He tunes into the sound of the wind and the leaves. His fingers tap the arm of the chair, that same spidery finger exercise we remember from many years ago.*

Shadows lengthen as hours pass . . .

His fingers continue the same exercise. Finally, they stop. DAVID *blinks. He has heard something. Or has he?*

139a INT. PSYCHIATRIC HOSPITAL CORRIDOR/MEETING ROOM. DUSK.

Shuffle shuffle go DAVID*'s feet on the cold, waxed floor, dragging a trail.* DAVID *inches down the deserted corridor, a cigarette dangling from his lips. He stops at the door of a locked room and looks in.*

His POV – the room is deserted, chairs stacked against a wall, shutters closed to the late afternoon sun. On the bare floor stands a piano.

New angle. DAVID *stares at it from the other side of the pane of glass, trance-like.*

Wide shot. At the far end of the corridor, DAVID *hasn't*

moved, still he stares into the room. A NURSE
approaches.

NURSE: David, I knew I'd find you here.

DAVID: Nurse, I've been a bit naughty again haven't I? I
    misbehaved, is that it?

NURSE: Come on, David.

*She ushers him away, down the sparse corridor, voices
fading.*

DAVID: Come on David, go-go-go, gotta-win-gotta-win –
    Come on, whooahh . . .

140 INT. PSYCHIATRIC HOSPITAL BATHROOM. NIGHT.

DAVID *is in the bath staring at the dappled effect of the
water reflected off the ceiling. He mumbles something
then lies there thinking. In his head, the sound of a few
fleeting notes from the past . . . a piano somewhere, or
is it?*

142 INT. PSYCHIATRIC HOSPITAL CORRIDOR/MEETING ROOM.
DAY.

DAVID *shuffles along the long corridor we saw him in
earlier. He follows the sound of piano playing. He
arrives at the door of the meeting room. It's open.
Inside, several patients dance to the tune 'Daisy' while
others do abstract activities.* DAVID *shuffles through
them, towards the person playing the piano.*

BERYL *is a matronly figure with a warm smile which she turns on to this poor creature,* DAVID, *who perches next to her. She goes to turn her music but he beats her.*

BERYL: Oh! So you can read music?

DAVID: Kind of, kind of, perhaps I could turn over a new leaf. Whooooah.

DAVID *rests his head on her shoulder. She plays on.*

BERYL: My name's Beryl Alcott. What's yours?

DAVID: Alcott Beryl, Alcott's a lot like Helfgott; it's true, it's true.

BERYL: Helfgott?

DAVID: That's it! Ridiculous! Would you believe it means 'with the help of God', Beryl. Incredible!

BERYL: What's your first name, Mr Helfgott?

DAVID: Incredible Beryl, first things first Beryl, it's David. How does that sound?

She stops playing – quite clearly stunned.

BERYL: You're David Helfgott?

DAVID: That's right, Beryl, that's right –

BERYL: I used to watch you win all those competitions.

DAVID: Ah well, win some, lose some. Can't lose them all, Beryl; it's not your fault. (*Touches the keys.*) Whooooah. (*Stops himself.*)

BERYL: I was quite a fan.

DAVID: So you don't mind if I turn for you?

BERYL: Do you still play?

DAVID: Mustn't play, mustn't play, doctor said, end in tears if I misbehave –

BERYL: You mustn't?

DAVID: That's right. Is that right? Might damage me, that's right isn't it, because it did once before – a long long time ago; that's the story, so what can you do, Beryl? Come on, Beryl, boldness of attack! (*She plays, troubled.*) The point is you've got to share and care and care and share and just behave. Isn't that right – that's right, that's good Beryl, give Beryl a medal!

143 INT. PSYCHIATRIC HOSPITAL CORRIDOR. DAY

BERYL *walks along with a* NURSE.

BERYL: What goes on in his head?

NURSE: God only knows.

BERYL: Is he schizophrenic or something?

NURSE: No, he just lives in his own little world; no trouble at all.

BERYL: Poor lost soul.

NURSE: He could leave tomorrow, but he's got nowhere to go.

146 EXT. PSYCHIATRIC HOSPITAL DRIVEWAY. A NEW DAY.

DAVID *shuffles out puffing on a cigarette, a battered suitcase in one hand, a plastic bag in the other hand. The door of an old Morris opens and* BERYL *calls out.*

BERYL: David.

He gets in the car.

BERYL: David, you know I can't abide smoke.

DAVID: Sorry Beryl, sorry.

He gets out.

BERYL: What are you doing?

DAVID: I'll walk, I'll walk –

BERYL: You don't know the way. Get in.

DAVID: I'll follow you. How does that sound?

He shuffles off.

BERYL: It's alright, God bless you, David.

DAVID *jumps into the car. As it drives off he hangs out the window with the cigarette in his mouth.*

DAVID: How's this, Beryl? Is this alright? Whooahhh!

The car drives down the drive, out the gates of 'Glendale'. Choral singing: Vivaldi's 'Gloria'

147 INT. CHURCH HALL. DAY.

Choir practice. BERYL *sings along in full voice with the choir as she plays the organ.* DAVID *turns for her.*

Vivaldi's 'Gloria' continues over:

148 INT. BERYL'S HOUSE. SMALL BEDROOM. DAY.

DAVID *sits up out of a dream, disoriented by his new surroundings.* BERYL *appears in the doorway, dressed in a nightgown with a glass of water and tablets for* DAVID.

BERYL: It's alright David, Beryl is here.

She sits on the bed. A framed picture of Christ hangs on the wall.

DAVID: Here-here never fear, but where's the nurse – the nurse, the sister Beryl?

BERYL: This is where you live now.

DAVID: It's true it's true, David's all better now, it's true. (*Guzzles the tablets.*) I'm fine, I'm fine, I'm fine? (*Mumbles on.*) That's right isn't it Beryl? Is that right? That's right . . .

She holds him, strokes his head tenderly.

BERYL: This is where David Helfgott gets right back on the rails.

DAVID: That's the story . . .

He innocently rests his hand on her breast . . .

149 INT. CHURCH HALL. DAY.

The choir sings on, straining their voices to the heavens.

150 INT. BERYL'S HOUSE. DAY.

BERYL *enters to complete chaos – the television blaring white noise, furniture, newspapers, dishes, spread high and low. Her reaction tells us it's not the first time. She picks her way through the fallout to the bathroom. The shower is running, the bath overflowing and* DAVID *is in it creating waves.*

DAVID: Don't you just love those big fat chords?

151 INT. CHURCH. DAY.

The choir, focused on salvation from somewhere up above, builds for a big finale. DAVID *turns for* BERYL . . . *then his hand continues onto her breast. She slides it away and hopes no one saw it.*

152 INT/EXT. BERYL'S CAR – TRAVELLING. DAY.

Clouds reflected in the windscreen. DAVID's *face stares out expectantly.*

BERYL: Mister Minogue is a lovely man, a real Christian gentleman; you'll like him, David. The botanical garden's just down the road, nice walk; and guess what – you'll even have your own piano.

She turns into a driveway, past a familiar sign: 'EDEN LODGE'.

155 INT. DAVID'S ROOM AT EDEN LODGE. NIGHT.

This is the same room from scene 18; the bed beneath the crucifix, the old TV and a battered honky-tonk piano. The radio is on full blast. DAVID *rolls a cigarette.*

156 INT. DAVID'S ROOM AT EDEN LODGE. DAY.

DAVID *plays a clamour of notes, puffing on a cigarette, the sound from the piano a muddle of confusion. Thumping from upstairs stops him. He sits on the floor, picks up some sheet music, peers myopically at it and then discards it.*

Pull back – new angle – looking down.

DAVID *surrounded by the debris of sheet music which covers the entire floor of the small room.*

It could be days, months or years he's been here.

158 INT. DAVID'S ROOM AT EDEN LODGE. NIGHT.

DAVID *plays the piano puffing on a cigarette, his head rolling back and forth. Loud thumping from above.*

VOICE: Shut up!

DAVID *stops.*

159 INT. DAVID'S ROOM AT EDEN LODGE. MORNING.

MINOGUE *enters with breakfast.*

MINOGUE: Top of the morning!

DAVID *is slumped at the piano, stupefied.*

MINOGUE: Let's make sure we eat our brekky today, David.

He turns the TV off and closes the lid of the piano, locking it.

MINOGUE: It's the last of the Chrissy pud'.

He puts a cheque in front of DAVID and hands him a pen.

MINOGUE: Look at you. You need to go out and exercise.

DAVID *signs the cheque.*

MINOGUE: Get some fresh air into those lungs of yours, David.

DAVID (*mumbles*): Exercise, yes Jim! Only the fit survive. That's right, isn't it – because the weak get crushed like insects, like grasshoppers.

MINOGUE *is already on his way out.*

160 EXT. BOTANICAL GARDENS. DAY.

JOGGERS *run past.* DAVID *mumbles, watches after them, then jogs off in their wake – a shuffle more than a jog.*

*He looks wonderfully absurd dressed in a tattered
greatcoat and a cigarette hanging from his mouth. He
runs up alongside a very serious* JOGGER *who gives him
the hairy eyeball then accelerates away. More joggers
run past in the opposite direction.*

DAVID: Whoooahhh!

DAVID *follows them, disappearing over a hill.*

161 EXT. CITY STREET. TALL BUILDINGS. NIGHT.

It's raining. DAVID *jogs in the shadows of the tall
buildings, aimless, lost in this deserted part of town.*

*Close-up – the only sound is his breathing. Each step is
heightened (slo-mo), the water glistens off his face. It's
more like a dream, with no sound at all now. He
presses on, as if drawn by an invisible force.*

*He stops under a bright street lamp, runs his hands
down his soaking face, then registers something – the
sound of a piano somewhere in the night.*

162 EXT. MOBY'S WINEBAR. NIGHT.

Rain-spattered glass reflects a blue neon sign. DAVID's
face enters frame as he looks into:

163 INT/EXT. MOBY'S. NIGHT.

This is scene 2 – from a different perspective.

DAVID's POV: *the last two patrons leave. The chairs are being put up.* TONY, *the waiter, draws the others' attention to* DAVID. DAVID *raps on the window. He is let in.* SYLVIA *comes over.*

164 INT. DAVID'S ROOM AT EDEN LODGE. DUSK.

DAVID *is unusually still. Seated at the locked piano, he stares at the red sky outside. A kaleidoscope of different sounds filters in, almost as if* DAVID *is singling them out one by one: traffic, children playing, someone coughing, a distant siren . . . then all goes silent.*

Close-up on DAVID; *something is on his mind. Finally, he whispers:*

DAVID: Chopin.

165 INT. MOBY'S. NIGHT.

SAM *sits at the bar with some friends. There are about twenty customers in all. He sees something:*

SAM: Sylvia, your stray dog's back.

It's DAVID, *walking towards the piano, nodding at the few customers.*

TONY (*to* SYLVIA): Do you want me to get rid of him?

SYLVIA: I'll handle it.

SAM ('*plays' to the customers*): Hey baby, give us a tune. What's it going to be?

Laughter, as DAVID *sits at the piano.*

DAVID: A tune – a tune baby, no worries.

He picks at a couple of notes.

SAM: Bravo! Encore!

DAVID *hooks his foot around the leg of the piano stool.*

DAVID: Encore! Encore whooahhh!

DAVID *drags the stool in closer.*

SAM: Sock it to us, Liberace!

More laughter. SYLVIA *approaches.*

Oblivious, DAVID *tinkles a note.*

SYLVIA: David?

She reaches out to touch his shoulder when – suddenly the piano erupts with the exhilarating sound of 'The Flight Of The Bumblebee'.

SAM *is dumbstruck –* SYLVIA *is astonished – everyone is spellbound.*

DAVID, *shrouded in smoke, bent double to the keyboard, delivers a stunning performance. Suddenly it's over. Stunned silence as the final notes resonate.*

Applause. Cheers. Whistles. Madness. Music.

166 INT. MOBY'S. DAY.

A bright flash. DAVID *– in a white tuxedo – is having his photo taken at the baby grand.*

*Cut to the photo in a framed poster – a flyer
advertising: 'The Classics at Moby's'.*

DAVID: Whoahhh!

SYLVIA *and* TONY *laugh.*

167 INT. MOBY'S WINEBAR. NIGHT.

DAVID *is at the piano – business is booming. Standing
room only at the bar; all tables full.* DAVID *laps it up,
fields requests, laughs and jokes with the crowd, as
eager as a puppy.*

168 EXT. HELFGOTT BACKYARD. DAY.

*Someone is reading a newspaper. We see the eyes –
aged, weary. It's* PETER *– mid-seventies. He's staring at a
newspaper article headed: 'REMEMBER WHO?' It's
accompanied by a photo of* DAVID *surrounded by
women at the piano; and inset is a photo of him as a
bright 12-year-old, headed: 'David Shines'.*

PETER *stares across the empty backyard . . .*

169 INT. MOBY'S WINEBAR. NIGHT.

An even bigger crowd, clapping, stomping, cheering.

DAVID: Thank you, thank you baby . . .

A bright flash as someone takes a photo.

DAVID (*blinded*): Oh, help, my glass, my glasses . . .

A girl holds DAVID's *wine glass to his mouth. Another replaces the stub smouldering on his lips with a new one.*

DAVID: Ah, a live one! A hot one baby!

CUSTOMER: Give us Beethoven's Fifth.

DAVID: Sure baby, no worries. Symphony or Concerto?

170 EXT. SYLVIA'S HOUSE. DAY.

The boot of a car is opened; a suitcase is lifted out.

SYLVIA: Excuse the garden, it wasn't covered in the maintenance order.

GILLIAN: It's a small price to pay for unwedded bliss.

SYLVIA: I must warn you, I have someone staying on weekends.

GILLIAN: He's not another Scorpio, is he?

SYLVIA: Very funny, Gills. He's a child prodigy.

171 INT. SYLVIA'S HOUSE. DAY.

GILLIAN *follows* SYLVIA *through a trail of chaos into the lounge, where the television is blaring, the radio and lights on, the sofa cushions spread all over; into the hallway where there are discarded clothes, a shoe, socks . . . into the bathroom.*

110

SYLVIA: David.

The shower is on, spurting like crazy, the floor is soaked, towels everywhere. SYLVIA *turns the shower off.*

SYLVIA: It's a madhouse. David!

172 BLUE SKY AND FLUFFY WHITE CLOUDS.

DAVID's *face floats dreamily up into frame. He's wearing a Walkman, eyes closed, his face plastered in zinc cream.*

173 IN THE KITCHEN.

The fridge is open, the radio on, food spread everywhere, burnt popcorn all over the stove, some of it still popping. GILLIAN *looks bemused as* SYLVIA *shuts the fridge.*

GILLIAN: You shouldn't have gone to so much trouble.

SYLVIA: Those kids were meant to be keeping an eye on him.

The KIDS *enter from the back.* JESSICA, *11,* ROWAN, *9.*

SYLVIA: Where in God's heaven is David?

174 DAVID SEEMINGLY 'FLOATS' UP INTO THE SKY AGAIN.

175 EXT. SYLVIA'S BACKYARD. DAY.

SYLVIA *and* GILLIAN *exit ahead of the kids.*

JESSICA: He's been hogging it.

ROWAN: For hours.

A look of amazement fills GILLIAN*'s face.*

DAVID *bounces up and down on a trampoline, listening to a Walkman and wearing a greatcoat which flies up with every bounce.*

GILLIAN *is drawn towards the odd figure on the trampoline.*

SYLVIA: David.

He turns around to see them, the greatcoat flying right up to reveal he's naked underneath.

DAVID: Is that you, Doctor?

SYLVIA *exchanges a 'can-you-believe-it' look with* GILLIAN.

GILLIAN: Doctor?

SYLVIA: David, I want you to meet someone.

DAVID: No more hot water, Sylvia, all gone. Where did it go?

He lands in front of them, rips the Walkman off.

SYLVIA: Gillian's a very dear friend of mine.

DAVID: A friendly doctor. I feel better already. Whoahhh!

GILLIAN: I'm pleased to meet you, David.

SYLVIA: Gillian's not a doctor –

DAVID: Not-a-doctor, sweet Sylvia.

SYLVIA: She's an astrologer –

DAVID: Oooh, a specialist, a heart surgeon.

SYLVIA: – she's from Sydney.

DAVID: An open heart surgeon.

SYLVIA: Don't be ridiculous.

DAVID: I'm ridiculous, ridiculous . . . um?

GILLIAN: Gillian.

DAVID: Gillian. That's it!

SYLVIA: If you ask Gillian nicely, she might just do your chart for you.

DAVID: Do my chart? Would she, would she do my chart?

GILLIAN: Of course, David.

DAVID: What's a chart, Gillian?

GILLIAN: An astrological chart.

DAVID: Oooh, the stars? I love the stars, they're astronomical –

GILLIAN: And the planets.

DAVID: Astronomical – the planets! Music for the spheres, the food of love, astronomical-gastronomical, whoaahh!

He hugs her tightly.

The food of love Gillian, whoaahh!

GILLIAN (*to* SYLVIA): What's he like when he gets to know you better?

176 INT. MOBY'S WINEBAR. NIGHT.

DAVID *ends a piece on the piano, to a packed house.*
GILLIAN *is seated at the bar, talking to* SYLVIA.

SYLVIA: So what does he do?

GILLIAN: He's an investment adviser; that's how I met him.

SYLVIA: So far so good. How serious is it? (GILLIAN *shrugs*.) Come on Gills, on a scale of one to ten.

GILLIAN *holds up her hand to display a chunky diamond ring.*

SYLVIA: God, that serious. So when's the happy day.

GILLIAN: I hate to rush into things.

SYLVIA *goes and serves a customer at the bar.*

GILLIAN *watches* DAVID *making his way through the throng, shaking all the hands offered to him, swigging from a wine glass, almost knocking over an ice bucket. His presence is infectious. He exits.*

177 EXT. STAIRS AT MOBY'S.

GILLIAN *looks up to the first floor where she sees a door ajar and cigarette smoke pouring out. She walks upstairs.*

178 GILLIAN'S POV – DAVID'S FLAT ABOVE MOBY'S.

He's crouched over a newspaper, its pages spread out all over the floor. He chain-smokes.

GILLIAN: Mind if I come in?

DAVID: Whoahhh the star doctor, entree, entree! Sorry, the paper, it's not your fault, it keeps getting bigger. Amazing. Amazing who you find when you're not even looking; he's here.

GILLIAN: Who?

DAVID: Roger-Roger-Roger, here!

On the entertainment pages, an advertisement for: 'Roger Woodward – In Concert' – and a photo.

DAVID: Roger the winner. Roger, he's a star, he's a hit-a-hit-a-hit; I need a hit, I need a hit.

He grabs the cigarettes.

GILLIAN: You've got one going already.

DAVID: Yes! One's more than enough. One two three the Rach 3, how's that sound?

He hums off a piece of paper.

GILLIAN: It started out being a letter.

There is some writing at the top which degenerates into musical annotations in DAVID'*s untidy scrawl.*

DAVID: A letter, Gillian. I think so, I think it's true. It seems to be true, is it true?

GILLIAN: 'Dear Professor Cecil, Royal College . . .'

DAVID: Of Music, Gillian, Royal College of Music. A mystery, it's a mystery –

GILLIAN: What is?

DAVID: – he only had one arm you see, it was a stroke, a stroke –

GILLIAN: The poor thing.

DAVID: – a stroke of bad luck. Whooah! It's not funny, it's sad, very sad, poor pussycat, his paw was damaged beyond repair and it wouldn't do as it was told, sad, sad pussycat. It was bad luck wasn't it, he was damaged, he was –

He nestles onto her shoulder.

DAVID: Am I – am I damaging you?

GILLIAN: Not at all. What's the matter, David?

DAVID: The matter – the matter, it started out being but it's all a bit of a blank-a-blank-a-blank because it's a long time ago, it was, a long-long-long-long-time-ago and that's the story Gillian, inexpressible, inexplicably inexpressible – (*Peers at the page.*) To express the inexplicable.

GILLIAN: Why not tell me what you want to say?

DAVID: Why not – why not? What don't I want to say? Whoooah, that's a hard one.

GILLIAN: It's quite simple. 'D.E.A.R. Dear . . .'

She writes.

DAVID: That's it, dear-dear-dear –

GILLIAN: Dear Cecil?

DAVID: Parkes, Cecil was Parkes, Mr Parkes. Touched his soul, Sergei Vasilievich himself, that wasn't too bad was it, the Rach 3 in D minor? Hard as elephants, elephantine –

GILLIAN: 'Dear Mr Parkes . . .'

DAVID: Long time, whooah such a long time –

GILLIAN: 'It has been such a long time.'

DAVID: It has – it has –

GILLIAN: 'And . . .'

DAVID: And-and-and-I hope. '*Hope*', Gillian, hope, how does that sound?

GILLIAN: Pretty good to me.

DAVID: 'I hope you remember me . . . and the Rach 3 . . .'

179 INT. TOWN HALL. NIGHT.

DAVID (V/O, *letter continues*): 'I am feeling much better now and have started playing again . . .'

117

A shiny black concert grand. Someone dressed in immaculate black tails plays. We do not see who just yet.

DAVID'S VOICE (*continues*): '. . . and I would very much like to play for you again one day, more than anything in the world, Mr Parkes. I should like that very much. I hope you are well. Ah, well, what can you do? Looking forward to seeing you again one day. Yours, David Helfgott.'

Reveal – the pianist is ROGER WOODWARD, *a face we recognise from all those years ago. In the audience* DAVID *nestles into* GILLIAN'*s arm.*

180 EXT. TOWN HALL. STAGE DOOR. NIGHT.

A crush of fans surrounds WOODWARD *as he exits. Nearby –* DAVID *and* GILLIAN.

DAVID: Roger the winner. He won, I lost –

GILLIAN: Just because you didn't win that doesn't mean you're a failure.

DAVID: No, Gillian, and just because you lose, doesn't mean you're a winner, does it? Whoahhhh!

WOODWARD *drives off in a taxi, past* GILLIAN *and* DAVID.

GILLIAN: Why do you think people come to Moby's –

DAVID: For the food, the mangiare.

GILLIAN: And the music, to hear you.

DAVID: Yes – yes but it's not very filling, it's not, because you can't eat the music can you; not very, not at all, not at all – got to keep on playing Gillian, gotta keep on playing that piano, I'll get it right yet –

GILLIAN: What do you mean?

DAVID: – S'right Gillian. I mean, I mean I got it right before didn't I? Can't let everyone down, can't – can't eat the music at Moby's.

She sees his yearning as he watches after the taxi.

DAVID: Ah well Roger, well done Roger . . .

181 EXT. SYLVIA'S HOUSE. DAY.

DAVID *hugs* GILLIAN, *buries his head on her shoulder. He's soaking wet, a towel wrapped around him.*

SYLVIA: Smile, David.

DAVID: I am, Sylvia.

SYLVIA: At the camera. Here!

She takes a photo of GILLIAN *and* DAVID.

SYLVIA: Time to go.

DAVID: Ah well, what can you do?

SYLVIA: David, look on the bright side –

DAVID (*overlaps*): The bright side, the silver lining.

SYLVIA: – You'll see Gillian again one day.

119

GILLIAN: Life goes on.

DAVID: It does – it does, is that what it does?

GILLIAN: Of course it does.

DAVID *holds onto* GILLIAN. SYLVIA *heads for the car with the suitcase.*

SYLVIA: Come on David, she has to go.

DAVID: Little wrigglies to look after.

GILLIAN: Hardly, my kids are all grown up. It's just little old me.

DAVID: I never grew up, I grew down. It's just me. Whoaaah! Bit of a handful. Bit of a handful, Gillian.

She gently touches his face.

GILLIAN: Shhh.

DAVID: Softly, softly.

He touches her face like a child and smiles.

DAVID: Will you marry me?

A moment. GILLIAN *is astonished.*

GILLIAN: It wouldn't be very practical, David.

DAVID: Practical? No, of course not, but then again, neither am I, Gillian, not very practical at all.

SYLVIA *(from the car)*: You'll miss the plane.

GILLIAN: That's very sweet of you David. I don't know what to say.

DAVID: The stars Gillian darling! Ask the stars!

182 INT. SYLVIA'S CAR. TRAVELLING. DAY.

SYLVIA: He's such a sweetie, isn't he?

GILLIAN – *clearly touched – casts a wistful look back at* DAVID, *waving like mad, receding in the distance as the car drives away.*

183 EXT. MOBY'S. NIGHT.

Someone's POV *from across the street as* DAVID *exits. Inside,* SYLVIA *and* TONY *put up chairs.* DAVID *shuffles up the stairs to the first floor flat, above the neon sign.*

184 INT. SMALL FLAT ABOVE MOBY'S. NIGHT.

Blue neon pulsates in the window. DAVID *has his head in the fridge. He hears the door.*

DAVID: Mangiare, sweet Sylvia –

He turns and drops a can of orange juice, not expecting to see – PETER *at the open door, large as life. Silence.*

PETER: Hello David.

DAVID: Daddy, hello Daddy . . .

He breaks off, picks the tin up, puts it on the bench.

PETER: Are you well, David?

DAVID: Well, well, Daddy, couldn't be better.

He wrings his hands, a confusion of nerves. He deflects.

DAVID: But the lids, can't open them, something wrong . . .

He fumbles through several other cans on the bench.

PETER: What could be wrong?

DAVID: It's a mystery, a mystery.

PETER *opens the top drawer, then the next and finds an opener.*

PETER: Watch.

He pops open a can and smiles, trying to be warm.

PETER: You see how easy it is?

DAVID: Yes, Daddy. Yes I do. Couldn't be easier, could it.

He mumbles on.

PETER *watches him, then tears his eyes away because the pain of it all is too much. He looks around.*

PETER: Do you realise what an opportunity you have here?

DAVID: Opportunity, opportunity of a lifetime . . .

PETER: You are very lucky.

DAVID: A very lucky boy, that's right, isn't it? Mustn't ever forget . . . (*Trails off.*)

Silence. PETER *hugs* DAVID, *then lets him go. Pause.*

PETER: You know David, when I was a boy, I had a

violin. It was a beautiful violin. Do you know what happened to it, David?

Pause.

DAVID: What happened to it? No Daddy . . . no idea, what happened, no . . .

PETER *is crushed, suddenly burdened with the weight of enormous loss.* DAVID *rummages in the cupboard for a glass, mumbling.*

DAVID: The thing is, um, have to be fit, to survive, to stay alive. That's right isn't it?

When he turns around, PETER *is gone. But there is something on the floor.* DAVID *picks it up. It's the gold medal he won in London. He studies it blankly then crosses to the window.*

185 INT/EXT. DAVID'S FLAT. STREET BELOW. NIGHT.

POV – *on the street below.* PETER *walks away, into the shadows – a solitary, doomed figure. He disappears into the night.*

DAVID: Good night Daddy.

186 INT/EXT. GILLIAN'S HOUSE. DAY.

A computer screen. The following is typed in.

'DAVID HELFGOTT – DATE OF BIRTH . . .'

GILLIAN *taps away. She rummages on her desk for her*

notes, then pauses to look at the photo of her and
DAVID *pinned on a cork board amidst postcards and*
other paraphernalia.

She can't stop thinking about him.

Cut to GILLIAN *standing on her balcony, lost in her*
thoughts. New angle – from inside. The television is
reflected on the glass door. We hear:

REPORTER: He grew up in the spotlight from an early
     age. By his mid-teens he was a six-time winner of
     the State finals of the ABC Instrumental and Vocal
     Competition, his virtuosity on the keyboards recog-
     nised by such luminaries as Barenboim, Vasary and
     Isaac Stern, who encouraged him to study overseas.

A close-up of the television.

REPORTER: At the age of 19, David gained a scholarship
     to the famed Royal College of Music in London, a
     remarkable achievement for the son of a working-
     class Polish immigrant. On the verge of international
     acclaim, he suffered a major breakdown and was
     institutionalised but his love of music never dimmed –

DAVID: The thing is music will always be your friend,
     that's right isn't it Daddy said – always, always; it's
     very noble music is, ve-ery nobling kind of, and it
     enables you to be ennabled, so that's nice isn't it, to
     have a friend –

Reveal GILLIAN *now watching the television up close,*
absorbed by the shimmering image of DAVID.

DAVID (*continues*): – because life goes on, it goes on

125

doesn't it – and well, you see if something goes wrong and amiss, well what can you do because it goes on and you just have to keep trying, you have to unravel it somehow, is that right? That's right. It's never too late to be better.

DAVID's *face radiates from the screen.*

187 INT. GILLIAN'S STUDY – NIGHT.

GILLIAN *works in the blue glow of her computer screen, tapping in astrological information from star charts. She stops and absently toys with the ring on her finger. She hits a key and waits for the chart to come up. In her hand, she discovers she has removed the ring.*

The screen lights up with an astrological map of the universe.

188 AN UNREAL BLUE. UNDERWATER.

Moving through it.

189 RESUME.

GILLIAN *absorbs the details of* DAVID's *astrological chart.*

190 UNDERWATER.

DAVID *struggles for the surface, the air escaping from his lungs.*

Cut to a shimmering image of PETER *against the blue sky, seen through the water's surface, smiling at camera.*

Cut to DAVID *sitting up in bed, in a sweat. We are in:*

191 INT. DAVID'S FLAT ABOVE MOBY'S. NIGHT.

The blue neon flashes, like in a dream. DAVID *is confused. The phone rings. He picks it up but doesn't say anything.*

192 INT. GILLIAN'S STUDY. NIGHT.

GILLIAN (*on the phone*): Hello . . . David? It's Gillian. David are you alright?

193 INT. DAVID'S FLAT ABOVE MOBY'S. NIGHT.

DAVID (*on the phone*): Um, yes, kind of.

GILLIAN: What is it?

DAVID (*oblivious*): It's a mystery, is that it? Not a tear you see, couldn't shed a tear –

GILLIAN: What do you mean, what's happened?

DAVID: No tears for the man of steel.

194 EXT. GRAVEYARD. DAY.

A headstone: 'PETER HELFGOTT'. GILLIAN *is with* DAVID *at the simple grave site.*

127

GILLIAN: What do you feel?

DAVID: Nothing . . .

GILLIAN: Nothing at all?

DAVID: Well . . . I'm shocked, stunned and completely amazed – how does that sound? My fault, all mine, all mine –

GILLIAN: You can't go on blaming yourself for everything that's happened.

DAVID: Can't go on blaming yourself, no Gillian and you can't go on blaming Daddy because he's not here any more.

GILLIAN: But you are.

DAVID: I am here, it's true – it's true, life goes on, is that right, Gillian, is that it?

GILLIAN: Yes!

DAVID: It does, it does – whoahhh, forever and ever it goes –

GILLIAN: Not forever.

DAVID: No-no, never forever, not quite, the point is it's not all lamb loin chops is it but it goes on and you just have to keep going too, you can't give up – can't give up.

GILLIAN: Certainly not –

DAVID (*overlaps*): Certainly not –

GILLIAN: – every time that blooming Saturn comes along and gives us a bit of a jolt.

DAVID: The stars Gillian.

GILLIAN: Everything has its season.

DAVID: It's a mystery, it's a mystery –

GILLIAN: There's always a reason.

DAVID: And we just need to seize the reason for the season.

GILLIAN (*laughs*): Bravo!

Cut to wide shot. They walk off, through the panorama of endless graves. As they continue away we hear joyous singing: 'Funiculi, Funicula'. It continues over:

195 EXT. GARDENS. DAY.

The wedding! DAVID *kisses* GILLIAN *endlessly in front of a gathering of friends and family, including* SYLVIA, TONY, RACHEL, LOUISE *and* SUZIE.

CELEBRANT: Let her breathe, David.

DAVID *hugs the celebrant.*

DAVID: I won't kiss you. It's alright, I won't kiss you too.

CELEBRANT: I should hope not!

196 INT. MOBY'S. DAY.

Singing. Dancing. Celebration! Several OPERA SINGERS *accompanied by* DAVID *chorus for the big finale of 'Funiculi Funicula'.*

SYLVIA *grabs* GILLIAN *and gives her a kiss.*

SYLVIA: Of course you realise you're crazy. Not that I'm not deliriously happy for you both.

GILLIAN: You know me, I hate to rush into things.

SYLVIA: Madness, honestly Gills, that's the only way to describe it, absolute bloody madness.

GILLIAN*'s eyes haven't left* DAVID.

GILLIAN: No . . . It's a mystery.

SYLVIA: So what do the stars say?

GILLIAN: Turmoil.

SYLVIA: I could've told you that.

197 EXT. THE NEW HOUSE. DAY.

A baby grand hovers in mid-air, descends slowly to the upstretched hands of removal men below. There's a 'Sold' sign in front of the house. GILLIAN *directs several other men carrying boxes etc, past a swimming pool, into the rear of the new house.*

The piano touches down; DAVID *starts to play it immediately. The men continue with their work – to the accompaniment of Mozart.*

131

198 INT. BEDROOM. DAY.

A chaotic jumble of furniture and boxes. We find our way through it, to GILLIAN *and* DAVID *curled up in bed together . . . actually on a mattress on the floor.*

DAVID: Sorry Gillian, did I damage you?

GILLIAN: Far from it.

DAVID: You made a noise –

He moans, mimicking her. GILLIAN *laughs.*

GILLIAN: David.

DAVID: David the Destroyer.

GILLIAN: Oh yes, Attila the Hun. David darling, I'm not damaged.

DAVID: That's right. Like me. I wasn't always was I, not when I was young –

He grabs a cigarette.

GILLIAN: What was there is still there, inside you.

DAVID: Is it Gillian darling, is that where it is? Can you see it?

GILLIAN: Of course I can.

DAVID: Whooah Gillian can see it, no one else can because they think, 'oh poor David, poor pity God didn't help him', I know, the thing is I know because I live here all the time, inside the damage inside –

She plucks the unlit cigarette from his lips.

GILLIAN: Not any more kiddo, starting now.

They kiss passionately.

199 EXT. WINTERY BEACH. DAY.

It's deserted all except for GILLIAN – *reading on the sand – and* DAVID *frolicking in the shallows.* GILLIAN *smiles as* DAVID *waves madly. She waves back. He runs along and dives under the water.*

200 UNDERWATER. DAZZLING SHAFTS OF SUNLIGHT.

DAVID *rises up towards the surface where we see pages floating on the water. It's music.* DAVID *breaks the surface and breathes the air, like he's been reborn. We are at:*

201 EXT. SYLVIA'S HOUSE. POOL. DAY.

DAVID *is surrounded by pages of music floating in the pool.* GILLIAN *exits the house.*

GILLIAN (*sees the music*): Oh no, poor Ravel.

DAVID: Poor Maurice, all unravelled.

GILLIAN: It's nearly time to get ready.

DAVID: Can I swim some more, darling.

GILLIAN: Ten minutes, swim the Campanella. That should do it.

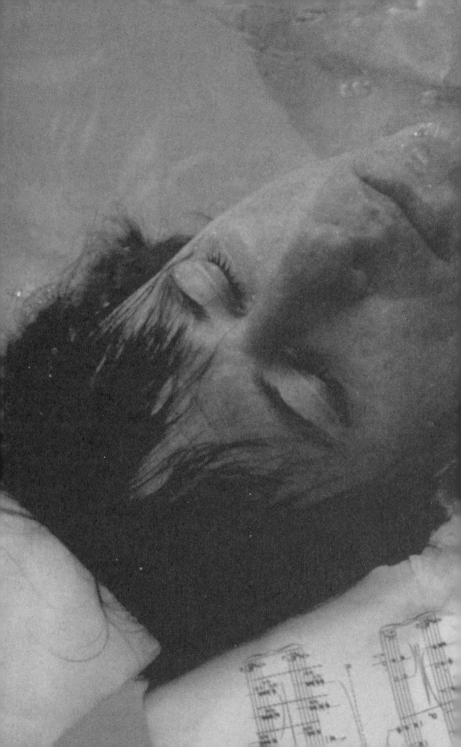

202 INT. SYLVIA'S HOUSE. LOUNGE. DAY.

GILLIAN *frantically dries the soaking music with a hairdryer.* ROWAN *and* JESSICA *help with the aid of a fan.*

DAVID (*buttoning his shirt*): It won't work, Gillian darling.

GILLIAN: Keep trying. Damn, page 15's missing.

SYLVIA (*to the kids*): Will you two go and get ready!

DAVID: The cadenza!

203 EXT. POOL. DAY.

GILLIAN *peels the lost page off the pool filter.*

GILLIAN: Gotcha!

204 INT. SYLVIA'S HOUSE. LOUNGE. DAY.

DAVID – *all done up in tuxedo, meticulous from his bow-tie down to his:*

GILLIAN: Odd shoes! Your first concert in years and you
   wear odd shoes?

DAVID: I'm a sausage.

GILLIAN: You certainly are. Sit.

She undoes the laces.

Up straight.

He does a parody of good posture.

DAVID: Sit up straight. Stupstraight . . .

He starts to slump as GILLIAN *does his lace.*

GILLIAN: Relax.

He sits bolt upright.

DAVID: Relax! Must learn to relax.

GILLIAN (*kisses him*): Perfect.

204a INT. CONCERT HALL. NIGHT.

A full house gives an ovation. Onstage, DAVID *stands by the piano, mopping his brow. He shuffles across the stage bowing again and again to cries of 'Bravo' and 'Encore'.*

In the audience there are many faces we recognise. SUZIE *is there, with* RACHEL *and* LOUISE. *Another face from the past is* BEN ROSEN. *There are many patrons from the winebar as well as* SYLVIA *and her* KIDS.

GILLIAN: Ladies and Gentlemen – David Helfgott.

He shies behind GILLIAN *and cuddles her, both hands on her breasts. Laughter. She walks him to the front of the stage, the ovation resounding around the hall. She hugs him.*

GILLIAN: They want an encore, David.

DAVID: Oh do they darling?

GILLIAN: What are you going to do?

DAVID: I'm going to win!

The audience stands, row after row applauding. DAVID *brings his hands up over his eyes, full of childlike wonder, overwhelmed.*

DAVID: Whooah!

The sound of applause continues into:

205 INT. RCOM. CONCERT HALL. DAY.

The scene of DAVID's *triumph all those years ago. The applause fades to silence as we find* ADULT DAVID *on the stage of the deserted concert hall, sitting at the grand piano – a cover over it now – lost in his thoughts.*

STUDENT'S VOICE: Excuse me?

The STUDENT, *an anxious 18-year-old, stands in the auditorium clutching an untidy armful of books.*

ANXIOUS STUDENT: Excuse me, have you finished? I really
    need a piano.

DAVID *considers him for a moment, then smiles, amused by something familiar that flickers in his mind. Over this the lyrical passage from the Rach 3 fades in, from:*

206a INT. RCOM. PRACTICE ROOM. DAY.

Pull back slowly to reveal we are in PARKES' *elegant old practice room and* ADULT DAVID *is at the piano,*

immersed. The camera drifts past him to reveal GILLIAN; *and seated next to her is* PROFESSOR PARKES, *older, quite frail but still with that same sparkle in his eye as he listens to* DAVID.

DAVID *performs for his old professor, full of joy.*

He has finally arrived.

DAVID: That wasn't too bad was it Professor?

PARKES: Not too bad at all, David.

DAVID *smiles . . . he plays on.*

DAVID: Shhh, softly softly, new story . . .

PRODUCTION BACKGROUND

The first ray of a light which was to change his life hit director Scott Hicks in 1986, when he noticed 'a tiny newspaper story' about an eccentric pianist called David Helfgott.

Helfgott's performances in a lively Perth restaurant, where he amazed and delighted diners with a classical repertoire of the highest calibre, were already famous. His curiosity piqued, Hicks set off to a Helfgott concert that very night, with no idea of the impact the experience was about to have on him.

What he saw in the modest concert hall that evening was to dominate his imagination for the next ten years. Helfgott was not only an endearing eccentric with a knack for showmanship. He was a classically trained concert pianist; an interpretative genius whose disappearance from the world stage, and subsequent reappearance in a Perth restaurant ten years later, was the stuff that dreams, and nightmares, are made of.

'I wasn't quite sure what to expect,' Hicks recalls of that first encounter, 'but from the moment David sat down and started to play he quite simply transported us all in the room. I was utterly captivated.'

After the concert Hicks felt compelled to meet both David and his astrologer wife Gillian. He already knew that here was a story he must make into a film. 'Of course they said, "Well who the hell are you?"'

It took Hicks over a year to win the couple's trust. 'But I persevered,' explains Hicks, 'because I was so inspired by

David. I couldn't get over the fact that he had endured such a tortuous and chaotic life and come out the other side in this remarkable relationship, an eccentric but still brilliant performer. I knew he was a wonderful story.'

The more he got to know David Helfgott, the more fascinated Hicks was by the man, not just the events of his tumultuous life. 'David is not driven by a need to control events,' he explains, 'and yet paradoxically, he has the power to stop the world in its tracks.'

Then of course there was the music. 'David's repertoire embraces the most widely popular romantic classics – Rachmaninov, Tchaikovsky, Chopin, Liszt – works which are not only brilliant, and tremendously challenging, but accessible to a vast audience, not just classical concert goers.'

Having nurtured a special relationship with David and Gillian, and reached agreement as to how David's extraordinary story could be translated to the screen, Hicks began researching and developing the story of the film he wanted to make.

In 1990 he called on Jan Sardi, a renowned screenwriter whose work he knew well, to take on the challenge of writing the screenplay. Sardi had been script editor on Hicks' 1989 feature, *Sebastian and the Sparrow*.

Sardi was immediately taken by Hicks' passion for the story. 'I very much wanted to be involved,' he recalls. 'But it's undoubtedly the hardest piece I've ever worked on. Not only did the story span three decades. When you're dealing with someone's life you tread that fine line between events that are known to have happened and your own creative licence. And of course the film must be entertaining. It must begin and end within 100 minutes and take the audience on an emotional rollercoaster ride.'

It was also important to both men, over the ensuing six years they spent perfecting the screenplay, that the film didn't read like a bio-pic. 'It's a film inspired by David Helfgott,' Hicks explains, 'and it uses a certain set of events and a certain character, but it's not a documentary, or a biography. It's a story in its own right.'

Hicks then approached Jane Scott to produce the film. Once again, Helfgott's story inflamed a seasoned industry professional's imagination. 'I'd known Jane for a long time,' says Hicks. 'She made it her own passion to raise the money and produce the film.'

'It was such a beautifully written piece,' explains Jane Scott, 'that I knew the commitment was going to be worthwhile. I fell in love with it. The trick was finding other people around the world who felt the same way about the project.'

It was not long before Ronin Films expressed their interest in becoming the Australasian distributor and the Film Finance Corporation began to talk of getting behind the project too. 'In the early stages this encouragement was crucial,' says Scott. 'It kept the project alive.'

Jane Scott had no way of knowing, however, that producing *Shine* would demand more than three years of her life. 'A low budget would have been easier to finance but the film would have been harder to make properly,' she explains. 'A higher budget meant going overseas for a bigger proportion of the finance, which was immediately more challenging.'

It also meant packaging the project with a strong cast and crew, drawing up hit lists and following every lead doggedly. 'There were a number of times I thought it was all coming together,' says Scott, 'only to have my hopes dashed. I began to think I'd never get the combination right, and I'd have to stop and get a proper job – one that paid!'

For Hicks too, the long years of purposeful investment in the idea of *Shine* were taxing. 'The project did come seriously close to having the lid nailed down two or three times,' he recalls. 'But every time it was almost financed, and then fell over again, I'd reassess. And I'd pick up the script and reread it again, and it said and did the same things to me, and somehow I'd find the resolve and the drive to stay with it.'

The persistence paid off when Jane Scott finally arrived at a combination which clicked. A deal with Pandora Cinema which acquired the international and US rights to the film ensued. 'Once Pandora came in,' recalls Scott, 'it triggered the rest. The FFC, and the BBC and SAFC, and Film Victoria. It was quite a mixed bag. At one point I was dealing with eighteen different lawyers.'

Once these negotiations had been settled, producer and director began putting the finishing touches to their plans to make *Shine* – a procedure every bit as tricky as the tinkering they'd been through so far.

While several big names had been attached to *Shine* throughout Jane Scott's years of carefully orchestrated pitching and packaging, the challenge was to balance intuition with pragmatism.

Hicks was convinced, for instance, that the character of David had to be played by an Australian, 'and by someone who could create an idiosyncratic character without caricature'.

In fact there was only ever one actor Hicks could imagine in the role, and he wanted to cast him before they had even met. But he was virtually unknown beyond the Australian stage.

'I'd seen Geoffrey Rush perform in the theatre over many years and watched him develop into an actor with no peer in Australia,' Hicks explains. 'He always seemed to play characters – like the fool in *King Lear*, and the lead in *The Diary of a Madman* – whose minds wander the fine edges of sanity.'

But for Hicks the decision was sealed in 1992 when he went to see the actor in *Uncle Vanya* at the Sydney Opera House. 'There were these big stills of him in the foyer, and he had the most magnificent hands. Fancy finding an actor with the capacity to play this role who also had beautiful hands! I mean if he had stumpy fingers it would have been impossible. David expresses himself through his hands. So I saw these stills, and rushed into the play, and witnessed a mesmerising performance. Even when he was doing nothing he was riveting to watch.'

Hicks had found the perfect Helfgott, despite the fact that most people who read the script said 'how will you ever cast this role!'

'But Geoffrey created a terrible dilemma for us,' Hicks recalls. 'At that stage the script was structured around two actors playing David. One was to play 18 to mid-30s–40s, the other the child. But there was no way Geoffrey could play 18. If I went with Geoffrey I had to get a middle David.'

So that led to the next problem – 'where would I find someone who looked enough like Geoffrey to make a believable younger version. It wasn't just a case of appearances, but eccentricity.'

While Hicks had known from the start he wanted Rush for the older David, he was also working on a hunch that Noah Taylor was the only person who could play the younger version.

'Geoffrey is about a foot taller than Noah, and looks quite different,' says Hicks, 'so it wasn't an immediately obvious choice. But I wanted to see them together before we abandoned the idea, so we brought them in and Noah was just brilliant. He had the right sensibility to be the young David.'

Hicks auditioned many young actors for the role, 'but I kept coming back to Noah,' he says. 'He's tough, and he's strong, but the camera also captures a fragility about him. He actually finds it irritating, because it's meant he is constantly cast as an adolescent.

'But he's such a mature performer he can reach back to 13 and then take David through that difficult transition into the world of confusion he experiences when he leaves his family, and then to the threshold of his breakdown – all with incredible poise.'

For Taylor, a musician like David Helfgott was a challenge he found he couldn't pass up. 'Emotionally it was so weird and hard to play a character ten years younger than me. I'm this haggard 27-year-old, so it was an unrealistic stretch. And it was so exhausting, such a responsibility to play someone you don't know, but you care for. David has more than survived. He brings so much joy to people.'

But Helfgott's eccentricities and his brilliance fascinated the young actor. 'Music is my ultimate passion,' he says, 'and David is possessed. It's almost as if he's tapped into some weird radio wave. Everything about him, his speech, his movements, is musical.'

Taylor was also intrigued to show 'how a fairly normal person can be pushed just a little too far over the edge and how that can suddenly make them snap and break.'

With the two hardest transitions in the hands of such consummate performers, the casting of the young David fell quite naturally to Alex Rafalowicz. 'It's quite amazing,' says Jane Scott, 'but Alex had something of both Geoffrey and Noah in his look. He gave a very tender portrayal and he was still only seven. Young children usually have a problem in focusing and don't always listen to what's being told to them, but Alex was very serious and took everything in.'

For the two older actors, the challenge of playing the same man at opposite ends of a devastating emotional crisis was not as daunting as it could have been. 'We'd worked together in *On Our Selection* as brothers,' explains Rush, 'and then here we were as the same person. We looked at my behavioural details that we thought would be useful echoes from one to the other – how David holds a cigarette, how he adjusts his glasses.'

But the actors were also helped considerably by the clever crafting of the script. 'By the time we see the adult David,' Rush points out, 'he's spent more than a decade in psychiatric institutions and has changed quite considerably, which justifies two actors playing the one character.'

With his major problem solved, Hicks and Scott accomplished a series of casting coups, which Hicks modestly attributes to the power of Jan Sardi's script. 'It was my calling card,' Hicks says. Just as the screenplay of *Shine* had wooed Jane Scott, it served as a powerful bait for talent as diverse as Geoffrey Rush, who committed to the project after reading the script in 1992, and Sir John Gielgud, who pronounced it 'quite extraordinary'.

'Sir John Gielgud had always been my ideal Parkes,' Hicks admits. 'For years I had fantasised about how marvellous it would be if we could actually shoot those scenes between Parkes and David in London, at the Royal College of Music.' As the film struggled through its various stages of development, the director was acutely aware that 'with every year that passed Gielgud was another year older'.

'And then finally there I was, gazing out of the window at the Royal Albert Hall, in the very same room I had visited two or three times over the years. But this time I turned around and there were the cameras, and Sir John Gielgud, Noah Taylor, Geoffrey Rush, and Lynn Redgrave, and the whole crew. A wash swept through me of joy that we were actually doing it.' In fact Gielgud celebrated his 91st birthday on the set of *Shine*.

Sir John for his part found Hicks 'most charming. Very young, very enthusiastic, but very quiet! I'm crazy about quiet directors like Resnais, Peter Greenaway and Scott Hicks! They don't make scenes and shout which is a great relief because all film sets are a bit of a hurly-burly, with lots of people coming and going. And suddenly, in the midst of this, you have to turn on a little scene. It's not easy and as one gets older it becomes more and more of a responsibility. I'm very thrilled though that I can still do it!'

He says the challenge of playing a musician with a withered arm, 'encouraging this strange Jewish boy to play the piano in England', was 'rather charming. And of course I had to remember not to use one of my arms all the time!'

Sir John was full of ideas about how his character would be, what he would wear,' says Hicks. 'He had amazing vitality and energy and a depth of complexity in his performance that few actors ever achieve. He was also very interested in my ideas.'

'It's to Scott's great credit,' Jane Scott points out, 'that he was able to work with this extraordinary cast with such confidence. Not everyone would be able to step up in front of Sir John and not feel a little nervous, but Scott was always very much at ease.'

'Every actor has their own style and traditions,' agrees Hicks. 'But particularly where a story is quite fragmented, you have to make sure they're all singing the same tune. Directing Sir John was a delight, like playing a finely tuned instrument.'

On the other hand, Hicks says, 'Noah works completely differently. He's a very instinctive performer. He'll always surprise you. You often watch him on set, and what he's doing seems very small and slight, and then you see it on the screen and you relive the nuance of it. That's what made him and Gielgud such an exciting combination.'

Geoffrey Rush was different again. 'Coming from a tremendous theatrical background, everything is based around the text with Geoffrey – learning every word and syllable,' Hick explains. 'Most of what Geoffrey did was inspired by David's speech patterns.'

'David babbles like a brook,' Rush concurs, 'but I found when I went over transcripts of his wonderful monologues, the rhythms and syntax were like poetry – as sophisticated as Shakespeare.'

For the critical role of Peter, David's father, Hicks faced another casting hurdle.

'I had to find an actor who could give me the subtext,' he says. 'People who read the script tended to respond to the darker side of the character. But we needed an actor with the pain in his eyes. You can't write that down, and that's why it needed a monumental actor to pull off the rage and fury. Many actors could have played the black part of Peter with no difficulty. But an actor who could communicate his own suffering, the victim in him, was rare indeed.'

Armin Mueller-Stahl, a favourite of Fassbinder's in the German cinema of the 1980s, who has more recently worked in Hollywood on such films as *Music Box*, was suggested by the film's Los Angeles casting director.

'I had seen Armin in *Music Box*,' says Hicks 'and I knew that he was powerful. But the attraction for me was that he lets that power seethe under the surface. He's never obvious. He has the ability to be utterly charming but you know underneath there's a time-bomb waiting to explode.'

For Mueller-Stahl the screenplay was the clincher. 'I had a few scripts on my table, but this was by far the best,' he says. It was the paradox of a love so strong it was destructive that fascinated him. 'I thought it was wonderful,' he says. 'As a child Peter wanted to play the violin but his father wouldn't allow it. So he tried to be the opposite of his father by pushing his son to be a great pianist. Because he's a very strong person, a true survivor, he pushes far too hard, which ultimately destroys David.'

'To his great credit, Jan Sardi is not someone to write in every nuance,' explains Hicks. 'As he says, that's interpretation.' And interpretation, Hicks found, was a very exciting process with an actor like Mueller-Stahl.

'The one thing Armin said to me when we met,' recalls Hicks, 'was that too many directors cut as soon as they think they've got it. He said sometimes it doesn't happen until after. And I really took that to heart because he would often hold a moment and it would turn into something else.'

All up, says Jane Scott, 'we had a very strong cast right through to the smaller roles.' Googie Withers was secured for the role of David's mentor and dear friend, the writer Katherine Susannah Prichard – a relationship which adds immeasurable warmth and richness to the film's emotional texture. 'It was a brief appearance and we were very fortunate she wanted to do it,' says Scott.

But the final coup was achieved when Lynn Redgrave agreed to take on the role of Gillian, David's wife. 'She was always at the top of the list,' recalls Scott. But when Hicks saw Lynn in her one-woman show in Houston, 'I knew immediately that she could play Gillian,' says Hicks. 'She had the range to be both tough and energetic, with a certain vulnerability and softness.'

The key was how Redgrave and Rush would work together, to create the powerful chemistry needed for the love story at the core of David's emergence from those long lonely years of doubt.

'Lynn and Geoffrey just clicked into something immediately and became a very powerful act together,' says Hicks.

'Both of us have a background in theatre,' agrees Redgrave, 'so we immediately spoke the same language. We talked through the permutations and possibilities of every little tiny moment. Geoffrey's a great actor,' she adds simply. 'He captured the essence of David. And he was just wonderful to work with.'

Of course, none of these performances would have registered if Hicks had not also chosen a cinematographer with the same instincts and passion as the actors.

'Geoffrey Simpson as Director of Photography was my first choice,' says Hicks. 'We'd worked together on a couple of projects, and we even went to school together. He's had a very fine career in Hollywood and Australia, and he's an absolute perfectionist.'

What Hicks particularly needed from his DOP 'was all in the lighting,' he says. 'We had to take the film into some very dark places, and chart the character's journey through that darkness, and out into the light again. And we agreed – let's not be frightened by shadows, dark corners and corridors. Lighting was the key to that.'

The other technique Hicks really wanted to exploit was a

lot of wide angle close-ups. 'A camera that close is very intrusive. It's inches from the actor's face. But it gives you a tremendously powerful image. We used it particularly with the younger David.'

Work so intense demands the stamina of a seasoned operator. In the fight scene with his father which drives David to leave his family, for instance, the camera was hand held throughout. 'It was very difficult for Geoffrey,' says Hicks. 'You can see the wobble in the frame because he was running out of energy to hold the camera. Then David breaks from the scene and Armin steps back into the light – a good actor will always know where the light is – and then he takes off his glasses. The phrasing is perfect. Totally unrehearsed. And we got the whole thing.'

Scenes such as these were captured in two or three takes. 'A lot of Australian films in the past have been technically perfect to an astonishing degree,' says Hicks. 'But powerful energy mustn't be rehearsed till it's dead. So one of the great challenges of this film was to catch the energy that pulsates through the script.'

'There were a number of scenes that were very like David's mind – quite fragmented,' Simpson says. 'So much of the camera work was quite extreme. For instance, in one of the scenes we get tighter and tighter and end with a frame composed of just one of David's eyes.' A special, absolutely silent camera, in fact, was used throughout the film for this reason.

With everything in place, the filmmakers embarked on an ambitious shooting schedule which began in London in April 1995. 'In London we had a lot of hassles especially because the cost of shooting there is phenomenal,' recalls Jane Scott. 'But once we'd decided we needed to shoot in London it was a matter of working out how.' Pre-planning from Australia was difficult, but the local councils, parking restrictions and London's notorious traffic were even more of a problem.

'It was hard to work out but we wanted to give it that

flavour of reality,' explains Scott. 'Seeing the real Albert Hall, the Royal College of Music and Trafalgar Square on screen gives the film so much dimension. Even though at the time it was extremely testing.'

Back in Australia seven weeks of principal photography followed at over 40 locations in and around Adelaide. The film was completed in January 1996.

While Hicks describes *Shine* as the story of 'an unlikely hero who nonetheless achieves the one thing we all desire: he finds his own place in the world, and someone with whom to share life, love and music' – at a personal level, the filmmakers lived their hero's journey during the making of the film.

'It was so scary when we finally got the money,' Hicks recalls, 'because everyone loved the script so much, and now I had to do it justice. Every single day of the shoot I'd get up and think it's never too late to stuff it up. Don't let anything get away from you!'

In fact, this determination was passed to each and every person who worked on *Shine* – from Hicks to Sardi to Scott. And then when the film was finished and everyone was pleased with the rushes, 'I said to our wonderful editor Pip Karmel,' says Hicks, 'here's a perfect script, wonderful rushes – now it's over to you. It was like passing the baton. The same happened with the music when I turned the edited film over to David Hirschfelder.'

This Olympian effort continued until the very day the film was screened at Sundance and the applause broke. At that moment the passion and care lavished on the project began to pay off – a result perhaps best summed up in the words of Steven Spielberg, who watched *Shine* and then said: 'At last, a great movie!'

Ruth Hessey

ABOUT THE CAST

NOAH TAYLOR – David as a young man

Noah Taylor is regarded as one of Australia's most talented film actors, noted especially for his leading performances in *The Year My Voice Broke* and its sequel *Flirting*, both directed by John Duigan.

Taylor has also starred in the features *Secrets, Lover Boy, The Nostradamus Kid* (for which he won the Sydney Film Critics' Award for Best Actor) and *On Our Selection.*

His acting career began at the St Martin's Youth Theatre under the artistic direction of Helmut Bakaitas, Malcolm Robertson and John Preston. His theatre credits include lead roles in *Pierrot Lunaire, Bloody Mama, The Grim Reaper, Baron in The Trees* and *Eric and Verna.*

Numerous television credits include the series *A Long Way From Home, Dolphin Boy, Bangkok Hilton, The Last Crop, Inspector Morse Down Under* and the BBC's *The Boys From the Bush.*

GEOFFREY RUSH – the adult David

In 1994 Geoffrey Rush received the Sidney Myer Performing Arts Award for his work in theatre. The award is offered each year to an individual who has shown himself to be a fine, original artist, capable of initiative and daring in his work. Numerous other recent awards and nominations place him at the peak of his 23-year career as an actor and director in over 70 productions.

In 1989 his performance as Poproshin in Neil Armfield's production of *The Diary of a Madman* (Belvoir Theatre) earned him the Sydney Critics' Circle Award for Most Outstanding Performance, the Variety Club Award for Best Actor and, a year later, the Victorian Green Room Award for Best Actor. This highly acclaimed production toured Moscow and St Petersburg before a triumphant return season at the Adelaide Festival in 1992.

Rush received Best Actor nominations in the Sydney Critics' Awards for the next three years – for his roles with the Sydney Theatre Company as Khilestakov in *The Government Inspector*, Astrov in *Uncle Vanya*, and John in *Oleanna*. In 1994 he was nominated as Best Supporting Actor as Horatio in *Hamlet* (Belvoir Theatre).

In 1975 Rush completed the Directors' Course (British Theatre Association) in London and then studied for two years at the Jacques Lecoq School of Mime, Movement and Theatre in Paris. On his return to Australia he played the Fool opposite Warren Mitchell's King Lear and co-starred with Mel Gibson in *Waiting for Godot*. He was a principal member of Jim Sharman's Lighthouse ensemble (1982–83). His major roles included Oberon in *A Midsummer Night's Dream*, Sir Andrew Aguecheek in *Twelfth Night*, Allen Fitzgerald in the world premiere of Sewell's *The Blind Giant is Dancing* and the title role in *The Marriage of Figaro*.

As a theatre director, he created *Clowneroonies* for the Queensland Theatre Company 1978; *The Small Poppies* (Adelaide Festival, 1986) which came at the climax of two years as Director of the Magpie Theatre for Young People; and for the Belvoir Theatre in Sydney, *Pearls Before Swine*, *The Popular Mechanicals*, *The Wolf's Banquet* and his own co-adaptation with satirist John Clarke of Aristophanes' *Frogs*.

Prior to *Shine*, he made only rare appearances in films: Gillian Armstrong's *Starstruck*, Neil Armfield's *Twelfth Night*, and as Dave in *On Our Selection*. Following *Shine*, he took a leading role in *Children of the Revolution*.

In the film Rush is frequently seen at the piano (although it is David Helfgott's playing heard on the soundtrack). 'I did all my own stunts at the keyboard! I already knew my way around a piano and I can read music. I had a fantastic piano tutor to assist me and I worked very hard. If you're going to play Hamlet you know you've got a big sword fight at the end, so you work on it. I was playing a concert pianist and so needed to pull off those moments that are similar to the sword fight!'

ARMIN MUELLER-STAHL – Peter, David's father

The brilliant German actor Armin Mueller-Stahl is perhaps best-known for his role opposite Jessica Lange in Costa-Gavras' drama, *The Music Box*. But he has many other films to his credit in international cinema, among them Barry Levinson's *Avalon*, Jim Jarmusch's *Night on Earth* and John Avildsen's *The Power of One*.

In his native (former) East Germany, Mueller-Stahl was a veteran of over 76 feature films and an even greater number of stage plays prior to his blacklisting, imposed by the government in retaliation for Mueller-Stahl's endorsement of the Biermann Resolution, a manifesto critical of the Erick Honecker regime. A Renaissance man (violinist, pianist, accomplished painter), he used this 'exile' to write the critically acclaimed *Ordered Sunday*, a book which chronicles this difficult period in his life.

After emigrating to West Germany in 1980, Mueller-Stahl resumed his acting career. 'I was almost fifty when I began my second career,' he says. 'Fassbinder called me and asked me to make *Lola* for him – that was an important step for me. I was very keen to concentrate on film. In the early part of my career I had performed on stage for twenty-five years in the same theatre in Berlin! After that I had become quite tired of acting and I still to this day have no desire to return to the stage.' *Lola* was followed by many other films in Germany including *Veronika Voss* also for Fassbinder; Istvan Szabo's Academy Award-winning *Colonel Redl*; and Agnieszka Holland's *Angry Harvest* for which he won Best Actor Award at the Montreal Film Festival.

Mueller-Stahl later moved to Los Angeles where he now spends much of his time.

JOHN GIELGUD – Cecil Parkes

Sir John Gielgud is a highly distinguished and prolific performer who is considered to be one of the finest actors of his generation. A graduate of the Royal Academy of Dramatic Art in London, Gielgud played his first Hamlet in 1930 and quickly established himself as one of the most eminent Shakespearian interpreters of his time, as well as a respected director. He made his screen debut in 1924 in *Who is the Man?* and appeared in Hitchcock's *Secret Agent* in 1936 as well as several Shakespearian adaptations such as *Julius Caesar* in 1953 and Olivier's *Richard III* in 1955. Since the late 1960s he has increasingly appeared in character roles.

Other film credits include: *St Joan*; *Becket* (for which he was nominated for an Oscar for his portrayal of King Louis VI of France); *The Charge of the Light Brigade*; *Oh What a Lovely War*; *Portrait of the Artist as a Young Man*; *The Elephant Man*; *Arthur*; *Chariots of Fire*; *Gandhi*; *Scandalous*; *The Shooting Party*; *The Far Pavilions*; *Plenty*; *The Whistleblower*; *Bluebeard*; *Arthur 2*; *Prospero's Books*; *Shining Through*; *The Best of Friends*; *The Power of One*, and *First Knight* with Sean Connery and Richard Gere.

The more recent of his numerous television credits include the BBC's acclaimed series *Brideshead Revisited*; *Wagner*; *The Master of Ballantrae*; *Oedipus*; *War and Remembrance*; *Quartermain's Terms*; *A Man For All Seasons*; *Dante and Virgil*; *Scarlett*; and *Inspector Alleyn*. Comments Sir John: 'I also did a film called *Providence* for Alain Resnais which I thought was rather successful. I enjoyed *Brideshead Revisited* very much and also *Prospero's Books*, although it was very exhausting. Those three films are the ones I would say I'm most pleased with. *Arthur* was also great fun and came at a time in my life when I really didn't imagine that I would be wanted for a leading role. And what luck! I got my Academy Award for that.'

Sir John has also written three novels – *Early Stages* (in 1939), *Stage Directions* (in 1963) and *Distinguished Company* (1972).

LYNN REDGRAVE – Gillian

Lynn Redgrave is the youngest child of Sir Michael and Lady Redgrave and sister to Vanessa and Corin Redgrave. She is aunt to Natasha and Joely Richardson and to Jemma Redgrave, actors all. The Redgrave name now stands for five generations of fine actors.

Lynn Redgrave made her professional debut in 1962 in *A Midsummer Night's Dream* at the Royal Court Theatre. She then auditioned for Laurence Olivier who invited her to become a founding member of Britain's National Theatre where she remained for three years appearing in *Hamlet* with Peter O'Toole in the title role and her father, Sir Michael, as Claudius. Her numerous theatre credits include *The Recruiting Officer*, opposite Maggie Smith and Olivier; Zeffirelli's production of *Much Ado About Nothing*; Noel Coward's *Hay Fever*; *Andorra*, opposite Olivier; the highly acclaimed production of Chekhov's *Three Sisters*, opposite her sister Vanessa and niece Jemma (this was the first time that the Redgrave sisters had worked together on stage); *Mrs Warren's Profession* (for which she received a Tony nomination); *Aren't We All?*, opposite Rex Harrison and Claudette Colbert, for which she was nominated for a Drama Desk Award; and George Bernard Shaw's *Don Juan in Hell*, with Stewart Granger.

Most recently, she wrote her own acclaimed one-woman show *Shakespeare For My Father* which she describes as 'the most fulfilling and exciting thing professionally that has ever happened to me. I had no idea I could write until I sat down and wrote the play. I thought I had written a purely personal story, until I found that audiences greatly enjoyed it. Writing is now something I'm keen to do more of, but the next one won't be autobiographical.'

Redgrave won the New York Film Critics' Award for Best Actress for her performance in the title role of the 1967 film *Georgy Girl*, a comedy hit in which she starred with James Mason, Alan Bates and Charlotte Rampling. The film also brought her a Golden Globe Award and an Academy Award nomination.

Her other film credits include Tony Richardson's *Tom Jones* with Albert Finney; *Girl With Green Eyes*, opposite Peter Finch; *The Deadly Affair*, with Maximilian Schell; and Woody Allen's *Everything You Always Wanted To Know About Sex*.

Australia has always had a special connection for Redgrave: her grandfather, Roy Redgrave, came to Australia in 1907 under contract to J.C. Williamson's theatre company and remained until his death in 1922. As well as many plays, he took leading roles in many silent Australian films including *The Christian* (1911), *The Road to Ruin* (1913), *The Hayseeds* (1917) and finally, *Robbery Under Arms* (1920).

ABOUT THE FILMMAKERS

SCOTT HICKS – Director

Scott Hicks is an Emmy Award-winning director whose work encompasses cinema features, television drama and documentary series, as well as commercials and rock clips.

After directing a feature *Freedom* (1981) and a highly praised telemovie, *Call Me Mr Brown* (1985) starring Chris Haywood, Hicks wrote, produced and directed a children's feature, *Sebastian and the Sparrow* (1988), which won awards at three international film festivals.

Hicks also directed and co-wrote the acclaimed documentary series *The Great Wall of Iron*, an extensive portrait of the People's Liberation Army of China in the months prior to Tiananmen Square. This Beyond International/BBC Television co-production won the prestigious Peabody Award as Best Documentary Series broadcast in the U.S. in 1989 and became the highest-rating programme in The Discovery Channel's history.

The four-hour series *Submarines: Sharks of Steel*, which he also directed and co-wrote, broke the ratings record set for The Discovery Channel by his earlier work. In 1994 Hicks was awarded the Emmy for Outstanding Individual Achievement in directing for this series. As writer and director Hicks completed *The Space Shuttle*, and *The Ultimate Athlete*, both two-hour specials commissioned by The Discovery Channel.

JANE SCOTT – Producer

Jane Scott, since entering the film industry in the UK in the late sixties, has established a prolific production reputation for herself, both at domestic and international levels. The lure of film wrested her from a promising career in magazine journalism. Scott's initial film experience was provided by the British Film Institute, first in Distribution and then in Production, where she 'worked her film apprenticeship'. After three years with the BFI it was time to venture out into the world of independent production.

Her first association with the Australian film industry was through Bruce Beresford and *The Adventures of Barry McKenzie* in the early seventies, followed a year later by *Barry McKenzie Holds His Own*. Production roles on various projects saw Scott make many trips to Australia over the next few years.

A permanent resident in Australia from 1979, Scott's producer credits include *Crocodile Dundee* (dir. John Cornell), *The Boys in the Island* (dir. Geoff Bennett), *Top Kid* (dir. Carl Schultz), *On Loan* (dir. Geoff Bennett), *Echoes of Paradise* (dir. Phil Noyce) and *Goodbye Paradise* (dir. Carl Schultz). International television credits as producer include the award-winning BBC series *The Boys From the Bush* (dir. Rob Marchand and Shirley Barrett) and the U.S. ABC's Stephen King's *The Tommyknockers* (dir. John Power). She also line-produced *My Brilliant Career* (dir. Gillian Armstrong), *Stormboy* (dir. Henri Safran), *The Survivor* (dir. David Hemmings), Baz Luhrmann's *Strictly Ballroom* and the international smash hit *Crocodile Dundee*.

Scott served as a Director on the Board of the South Australian Film Corporation from 1989–1995.

Shine represents the culmination of an impressive twenty-five years in the film industry. Scott is currently developing several other film and television projects.

JAN SARDI – Screenwriter

Jan Sardi has a strong reputation as one of Australia's finest screenwriters for film and television.

Amongst Sardi's feature film credits are *Moving Out* and *Street Hero*, both of which were nominated for Best Original Screenplay by the Australian Film Institute and the Australian Writers' Guild; *Ground Zero*, which received nine AFI nominations, including Best Screenplay and Best Picture and was a finalist at the 1988 Berlin Film Festival; *Secrets*; and *Just Friends*, a telemovie which received the Best Film Award at the Chicago International Festival of Children's Films.

Sardi's television series credits include *Embassy*, *Phoenix*, *Mission Impossible*, and *The Man From Snowy River*. His telemovie credits include *The Feds* and *Halifax f.p.*

He is currently adapting a novel *The Notebook* for U.S. company, New Line Cinema.

In July 1996, Jan Sardi won two AWGIE awards – Best Screenplay for a telemovie (for *Halifax f.p.*) and Best Original Screenplay for *Shine*.

GEOFFREY SIMPSON – Director of Photography

Geoffrey Simpson, one of Australia's most successful directors of photography, is also known for the significant work he has done all around the world. He recently filmed *Somebody's Son* in Ireland, for director Terry George, which premiered at this year's Cannes Film Festival. Other film credits include *Little Women* for director Gillian Armstrong; Peter Weir's *Green Card*, shot on location in New York; John Avnet's *Fried Green Tomatoes*; Anthony Minghella's *Mr Wonderful*, starring Matt Dillon; Gillian Armstrong's *The Last Days of Chez Nous*; John Seale's *'Til There Was You*; and Avnet's *The War*, which featured Kevin Costner. Simpson began his career working on documentaries such as *The Migrant Experience*, *Nicaragua No Pasaran* and *Where Death Wears a Smile*. In 1981 he won the Golden Tripod ACS Award for the dramatised television documentary *Breaking Point*, which he followed in 1982 with a corporate documentary *Electricity* and the feature film *Centrespread*, both of which won Golden

Tripod ACS Awards that year.

A recipient of numerous accolades, he won the 1985 Golden Tripod ACS Award and Milli Award as Cinematographer of the Year for the feature film *Playing Beattie Bow* and won an ACS Merit Award in the same year for Scott Hicks' *Call Me Mr Brown*. *The Shiralee*, an Australian television mini-series, won him the Silver Tripod ACS Award in 1987, and in 1988 he won the Golden Tripod ACS Award for Kennedy Miller's tele-feature *Riddle of the Stinson*. Simpson then completed the acclaimed feature film *The Navigator*, directed by Vincent Ward, which won both the 1988 Australian Film Institute Award and the 1989 New Zealand Film & Television Award for Cinematography.

PIP KARMEL – Editor

Australian editor Pip Karmel is also an award-winning writer/ director. In 1993 she directed *The Long Ride*, winning Best Tele-feature at the 1994 Australian Film Institute Awards. In 1991 her short drama *Fantastic Futures* won several awards including the ITVA Grand Mobie and a Gold Award at the New York Film Festival.

A graduate of the Australian Film, Television and Radio School, Karmel's graduate film, *Sex Rules*, received wide acclaim at international festivals and won the Jury Prize at the 1990 ATOM Awards.

Karmel first worked with director Scott Hicks as First Assistant Editor on his 1985 tele-feature *Call Me Mr Brown* and went on to edit his next feature, *Sebastian and the Sparrow*.

DAVID HIRSCHFELDER – Music Director and Composer

David Hirschfelder is the musical genius behind Baz Luhrmann's acclaimed feature film *Strictly Ballroom*. In Australia the film was nominated for a staggering 13 AFI

Awards, and after being nominated in three categories at the British Film and Television Academy Awards (BAFTA), Hirschfelder took out the sole prize for Best Original Music. The soundtrack debuted in the Australian music charts at No. 6 and remained in the Top 10 for six weeks.

Hirschfelder has long been regarded as one of the key players on the Australian music scene. He first sprang to prominence in 1980, playing keyboards and producing for his jazz-fusion band Pyramid. He began composing theme music for television and won a Penguin Award for Best Musical Score in 1987 for *Suzy's Story*, a remarkable award-winning documentary. In 1990 Hirschfelder composed the music for the Channel 10 mini-series *Shadows of the Heart*, which was nominated as Best TV Theme at the APRA Awards.

Hirschfelder has worked as musician, songwriter, programmer and arranger on the John Farnham albums Whispering Jack, Age of Reason, Chain Reaction and Full House, as well as being Farnham's musical director on his numerous record-breaking tours. He also produced and performed on the Australian Cast recording of Jesus Christ Superstar (starring John Farnham) which debuted at No. 1 on the Australian music charts, went platinum on the first day and double platinum within eight weeks.

As a recording musician and producer, Hirschfelder has featured on albums by Peter Cupples, Little River Band, Colleen Hewitt, Vanetta Fields and Dragon. (He produced Dragon's album Bondi Road, which earned a gold record.)

At the 1993 ARIA Awards Hirschfelder was nominated as Producer of the Year for his production of the No. 1 song, Everything's All Right, sung by John Farnham and Kate Ceberano, adding this prestigious accolade to his already impressive list of achievements.

CREW LIST

Producer
JANE SCOTT

Director
SCOTT HICKS

Writer
JAN SARDI

Music
DAVID HIRSCHFELDER

Editor
PIP KARMEL

Director of Photography
GEOFFREY SIMPSON A.C.S.

Production Designer
VICKI NIEHUS

Costume Designer
LOUISE WAKEFIELD

First Assistant Director
**CAROLYNNE
    CUNNINGHAM**

Casting
**LIZ MULLINAR (Australia)
SHARON HOWARD FIELD
    (USA)
KAREN LINDSAY-STEWART
    (UK)**

Creative Consultant
KERRY HEYSEN

Sound Recordist
TOIVO LEMBER

Re-recording Mixer
ROGER SAVAGE

Production Manager
ELIZABETH SYMES

Production Coordinator
SERENA GATTUSO

Production Secretary
HEATHER MUIRHEAD

Production Runner
SCOTT HEYSEN

Producer's Assistant
CHRISTINA NORMAN

Production Accountant
CHRIS McGUIRE

Accounts Assistant
COLLEEN KENNEDY

Second Assistant Directors
**HENRY OSBORNE
GUY CAMPBELL**

Third Assistant Director
TOM READ

Second Assistant Director
    Attachment
JULIE BYRNE

Third Assistant Director
    Attachment
LEILAH SCHUBERT

Continuity
JO WEEKS

Location Manager
MAURICE BURNS

Location Assistant
JOSH MOORE

Unit Manager
ANDREW MARSHALL

Unit Assistants
TINA HENNEL
PAUL LIGHTFOOT
DEB HANSON

Camera Operator
GEOFFREY SIMPSON A.C.S.

Focus Puller
SALLY ECCLESTON

Clapper Loader
JASMINE CARRUCAN

Video Split Operator
RENEE HANNA

Second Unit Cameraman
DAVID FOREMAN A.C.S.

Second Unit Camera Assistant
CRAIG PHILPOTT

Second Unit Gaffer
GRAEME SHELTON

Boom Operator
SCOTT PIPER

Gaffer
TREVOR TOUNE

Best Boy
WERNER GERLACH

Electrics
ANDY SMITH
ROBERTO KARAS
RICHARD HYDE

Key Grip
JON GOLDNEY

Assistant Grips
SCOTT BROKATE
PETER SANTUCCI

Art Director
TONY CRONIN

Props Buyer/Set Dressers
ANDREW SHORT
ALICIA WALSH

Standby Props
LEROY PLUMMER

Art Department Coordinator
LOUISE CAMERON

Art Department Runner
PERSCIA BROKENSHA

Draughtsman
ADAM McCULLOCH

Greensman
BROCK SYKES

Art Department Attachment
JACQUI CANTY

Construction Manager
ARTHUR VETTE

Carpenter
KEVIN JARRETT

Scenic Artist
JOHN HARATZIS

Painters
BEN JOHNSON
JOHN SANTUCCI

Action Vehicle Coordinator
JON BLAIKIE

Costume Supervisor
JENNY MILES

Standby Wardrobe
NINA PARSONS

Cutter
SUE NICOLA

Costume Assistant
JENNY RAMOS

Costume Assistant/Cutter
MARRIOTT KERR

Costume Assistants
MONICA WILLIS
JEANETTE LUKE
ANGELA WINTERS

Make-Up Artist
LESLEY VANDERWALT

Hairdresser
PAUL WILLIAMS

Additional Hair/Make-up
FIONA REES JONES
LIZ DINGLE
RICK MARTIN

Stills Photographer
LISA TOMASETTI

Story Research & Development
JOHN MACGREGOR

Extras Casting
JAN KILLEN

Stunts Coordinator
RICHARD BOUE

Special Effects Coordinator
RAY FOWLER

Safety Report
BERNADETTE VAN GYEN

Unit Nurse
JENNY BICHARD

Publicity (Australia)
TRACEY MAIR

Publicity (International)
FIONA SEARSON (DDA)

Caterer
STEVE MARCUS

Catering Assistant
MELINDA PARKER

Assistant Film Editor
MARK ELLIS

Post Production Supervisor
SYLVIA WALKER-WILSON

Sound Effects Editor
GARETH VANDERHOPE

Dialogue Editor
LIVIA RUZIC

Assistant Sound Editor
MARTIN BAYLEY

Foley
GERARD LONG
STEVE BURGESS

Soundfirm Liaison
HELEN FIELD

Psychiatric Advisor
STEVE CROOK

Yiddish Advisor
SAL ALBA

Bar Mitzvah Advisor
RABBI FIGDOR

Assistant Musical Director
RICKY EDWARDS

Music Production Manager
PETER HOYLAND

Music Notation Manager
SAM SCHWARZ

Music Mixing Engineer
MICHAEL LETHO

Additional Music Engineers
ROBIN GRAY
ADAM RHODES
DAVID WILLIAMS

Assistant Music Editor
MICHAEL COSTA

Music Production Assistants
SANDY EDWARDS
STELLA O'MALLEY

Source Music Clearances
KIM GREEN
CHRISTINE WOODRUFF

Harpsichord Technician
VLADIMIR CHISHKOVSKY

Disklavier Technician
BRENT OTTLEY

Studio Technician
ROSS CLUNES

Orchestral Leader
ROBERT JOHN

Lawyer (Australia)
**GREG SITCH (Marshalls &
    Dent)**

Lawyer (USA)
**FREDERIC N. GAINES (Mayer,
    Glassman & Gaines)**

Completion Guarantor
FILM FINANCES INC.

Camera Equipment
**CAMERAQUIP (AUST) PTY
    LTD**

Laboratory (Shoot)
**CINEVEX FILM
    LABORATORIES**

Laboratory (Post)
ATLAB FILM LABORATORIES

Optical Effects
PAUL CROSS

Negative Matching
ROHAN WILSON

Laboratory (Liaison)
IAN ANDERSON (Cinevex)
IAN RUSSELL (Atlab)

Colour Grading
ARTHUR CAMBRIDGE

Post Production Sound
SOUNDFIRM

Music Recording
ADELPHIA STUDIO
ALLANEATON STUDIO

Titles
OPTICAL & GRAPHIC

UK CREW

Production Advisor
PAUL SARONY

Production Coordinator
HILARY BENSON

Production Secretary
SUSIE MENZIES

Production Runner
SARA MORRIS

Production Accountant
CHERRY FIDDAMAN

Cashier
LESLEY CAMPION

Continuity
SUSANNA LENTON

Location Manager
CHARLES HUBBARD

Assistant Location Manager
RIKKE DAKIN

Second Assistant Director
STEPHEN WOOLFENDEN

Third Assistant Director
TOBY COKE

Stills Photographer
MARK TILLIE

Art Director
DAVID McHENRY

Props Buyer/Set Dresser
JUDY FARR

Assistant Art Director
JOHANNA GRAYSMARK

Prop Master
PAUL PURDY

Standby Prop
PETER LOOBY

Dressing Prop
MIKE BARTLETT

Standby Carpenter
ALISTAIR GOW

Clapper Loader
LORRAINE LUKE

Camera Trainee
ALIX MUMFORD

Steadicam Operator
JAN PESTER

Focus Puller/Steadicam
SAM GARWOOD

Grip
BARRY READ

Gaffer
JOHN DONOGHUE

Best Boy
WARREN EWAN

Electrician
PETER ARNOLD

Generator Operator
TONY BURNES

Sound Recordist
JIM GREENHORN

Boom Operator
JOANNE STEPHENS-SMITH

Wardrobe Supervisor
ROS WARD

Wardrobe Assistant
IONA KENRICK

Make-up Artist
PAMELA HADDOCK

Make-up Assistant
SUE BLACK

Unit Drivers
HARRY SMITH
JOHN SMITH

JIM ATKINS
PAUL VENEZIA
CLIVE RANDALL
PAUL THOMPSON

Caterer
WOODHALL CATERING

Extras Casting
ROBERT SMITH AGENCY

Additional Casting
RAY KNIGHT CASTING

Costume Hire
MORRIS ANGEL & SON LTD

Laboratory
METROCOLOUR FILM LABS

MUSIC

WITH A GIRL LIKE YOU
Written by Reg Presley
© 1966 Dick James Music Limited
Performed by The Troggs
(p) 1966 Mercury Ltd London

WHY DO THEY DOUBT OUR LOVE
Written and performed by Johnny O'Keefe
© 1959 Victoria Music/MCA Music Australia Pty Ltd
(p) 1959 Festival Records Pty Ltd

POLONAISE in A flat major, Opus 53
Composed by Frederic Chopin
Performed by Ricky Edwards

FAST ZU ERNST – SCENES FROM CHILDHOOD Opus 15
Composed by Robert Schumann
Performed by Wilhelm Kempff
(p) 1973 Polydor International GmbH Hamburg

LA CAMPANELLA
From Violin Concerto in B minor by Niccolo Paganini
Transcribed for piano by Franz Liszt
Performed by David Helfgott

HUNGARIAN RHAPSODY No 2 in C sharp minor
Composed by Franz Liszt
Performed by David Helfgott

FLIGHT OF THE BUMBLE BEE
Composed by Nikolai Rimsky-Korsakoff
Arranged by Sergei Rachmaninoff
Performed by David Helfgott

GLORIA, rv 589
Composed by Antonio Vivaldi
Arranged by David Hirschfelder & Ricky Edwards
© Polygram Music Publishing/Mushroom Music

SOSPIRO
Composed by Franz Liszt
Performed by David Helfgott

NULLA IN MUNDO PAX SINCERA
Composed by Antonio Vivaldi
Arranged by David Hirschfelder & Ricky Edwards
© Polygram Music Publishing/Mushroom Music
Performed by Jane Edwards (Soprano)
Geoffrey Lancaster (Harpsichord) and Gerald Keuneman (Cello)

DAISY BELL
Composed by Harry Dacre
Arranged and performed by Ricky Edwards
© Mushroom Music

FUNICULI, FUNICULA
Composed by Luigi Denza
Arranged by David Hirschfelder & Ricky Edwards
© Polygram Music Publishing/Mushroom Music

PIANO CONCERTO No 3 in D minor Opus 30
Composed by Sergei Rachmaninoff
Arranged by David Hirschfelder
Performed by David Helfgott
© Polygram Music Publishing

PRELUDE in C sharp minor Opus 3, no 2
Composed by Sergei Rachmaninoff
Performed by David Helfgott
© 1994 RAP Productions, Denmark

SYMPHONY No 9 in D minor Opus 125
Composed by Ludwig van Beethoven
Arranged by David Hirschfelder & Ricky Edwards
© Polygram Music Publishing/Mushroom Music

APPASSIONATA SONATA, no 23 in F minor Opus 57
Composed by Ludwig van Beethoven
Performed by Ricky Edwards

PRELUDE no 15 Opus 28
Composed by Frederic Chopin
Performed by David Helfgott
© Revolver

Financed by The Australian Film Finance Corporation.
Developed and produced with the assistance of The South Australian
    Film Corporation.
Developed and produced with the assistance of Film Victoria.
Produced with the financial and marketing assistance of The
    Australian Film Commission. Produced in association with
    Pandora Cinema.

176